PROBLEM ZONES

PROBLEM ZONES

Margit Rudiger · Sabine Haberlein

The Sure-Fire
3-Point Program

Sterling Publishing Co., Inc.
New York

Library of Congress Cataloging-in-Publication Data

Rudiger, Margit.
  [Problemzonen. English]
  Problem zones : the sure-fire 3-point program / by Margit Rudiger and Sabine Haberlein.
      p.   cm.
  ISBN 0-8069-4247-9
  1. Obesity–prevention. 2. Weight loss. 3. Cellulite. I. Haberlein, Sabine. II. Title.
RC628.R8313 1998
616.3´9805—dc21   98-34949
                                            CIP

10 9 8 7 6 5 4 3 2 1

Published by Sterling Publishing Company, Inc.
387 Park Avenue South, New York, N.Y. 10016
Originally published in Germany by Falken-Verlag GmbH Niedernhausen/Ts under the title *Problemzonen: fester Po, straffe Schenkel, flacher Bauch, schmale Hüften*
© 1996 by Falken-Verlag GmbH Niedernhausen/Ts.
English translation © 1998 by Sterling Publishing Co., Inc.
Distributed in Canada by Sterling Publishing
c/o Canadian Manda Group, One Atlantic Avenue, Suite 105
Toronto, Ontario, Canada M6K 3E7
Distributed in Great Britain and Europe by Cassell PLC
Wellington House, 125 Strand, London WC2R 0BB, England
Distributed in Australia by Capricorn Link (Australia) Pty Ltd.
P.O. Box 6651, Baulkham Hills, Business Centre, NSW 2153, Australia
Printed in Hong Kong
All rights reserved

Sterling ISBN 0-8069-4247-9

Photo credits:

Cover: Transglobe, A. Schroeder. 1: Thomas von Salomon. 2–3: Michael Leis. 8: Freundin archive. 9: Michael Leis. 11–15: Freundin archive. 16: Biotherm. 18: Antje Hain-Pesel. 19: Gerald Klepka. 21: Biotherm. 22: Freundin archive. 23: Michael Leis. 24: Michael Leis; Tom Biondo. 25: Michael Leis. 26 & 28: Freundin archive. 29: Peter Pfander; Tom Biondo; free oil; L. Matzen. 30: Peter Pfander. 32: Hannelore Hopp. 33 & 34: Michael Leis. 35: Gerald Klepka. 36 & 39: VIP Aesthetic Rhine Park Clinic, Dusseldorf. 40: Michael Leis. 41: Tery Lang. 42: Freundin archive; Michael Leis. 44: Michael Leis. 46: Freundin archive (3); Michael Leis (1). 47: Michael Leis; Jürgen Schwopl. 48–49: Gik Piccardi (Peter Maltz, illustration). 50–51: Jürgen Reisch (5). 52–59: Gerald Klepka. 60 & 61: Freundin archive. 62: Jürgen Reisch; Gerald Klepka. 63: Gerald Klepka. 64: Tom Biondo; Gerald Klepka. 65: Jörg Steffens; Gerald Klepka. 66 & 67: Freundin archive. 68: Tery Lang. 69: Reebock. 70–71: Tery Lang. 72–77: Hannelore Hopp. Location: Kaifu Lodge, Hamburg. 78: Jürgen Reisch. 80: Prinz Health & Fitness, Munich. 81: Michael Leis; Freundin archive. 83: Gerald Klepka. 84: John Kelly; Gerald Klepka; Aldo Acqadro; Freundin archive. 86: Thomas von Salomon (2); Freundin archive. 87: Otto Rauser; Thomas von Salomon; Freundin archive. 88–89: Freundin archive. 90: Hannelore Hopp; Antje Hain-Pesel; Gerald Klepka. 91: Antje Hain-Pesel; Gerald Klepka; Hannelore Hopp. 92 & 93: Stock Food/Eising. 94 & 95: Stock Food/Eising (3); Harry Bischof (1). 96: Freundin archive; Stock Food/Eising. 97: Thomas von Salomon. 98 & 99: Freundin archive. 100: Gerald Klepka; Freundin archive. 101: Michael Brauner; Stock Food/Eising (2). 102: Stock Food/Eising (3). 103: Stock Food/Eising (2); Chris Meier. 104: Frank Herholdt/Tony Stone; Freundin archive. 105: Michael Brauner (2); Freundin Archive. 108: Yvonne Kranz; Freundin archive (2). 109: Chris Meier; Freundin archive. 110: Tom Biondo; Freundin archive (2). 111 & 112: Freundin archive (3). 113: Freundin archive (2); Thomas von Salomon. 114: Stock Food/Eising; Otto Rauser; Freundin archive (2). 115: Freundin archive; Stock Food/Eising. 116: Roger Spiess; Freundin archive (3). 117: Freundin archive; Stock Food/Eising. 118 & 119: Freundin archive. 120: Michael Leis. 121: Tom Biondo. 123: Michael Leis.

Problem zones are the areas of the body which most people are not happy with. They usually refer to the section from the upper body down to the lower parts of the body: too thick thighs and hips, or too large stomachs and buttocks. Of course, "too thick" and "too large" are relative terms based upon how each person perceives his or her own body. In general, women are more concerned with these problem zone areas, which, after all, men also have. This is probably because of the image of the physically "ideal" woman, with narrow hips and thighs, shown in advertising and fashion magazines.

Although we do not intend to alter your vision of what the physical ideal should be, we do feel that it is always good to be working towards a better body. And the key to that is through exercise and proper nutrition. Anyone who does some form of regular exercise routine and eats conscientiously will see physical improvements, especially at their problem zones. In addition to looking good, exercise and nutrition means being in better health, which improves your overall state— from your mood to your energy level.

So don't waste your energy disliking how you look. Rather, put it to constructive use. Not only will you look better, but you will also be healthier and have more self-confidence.

Anti-cellulite creams: Activating the skin's metabolism

Massage and sea salt bath: Smoothing and removing tissue sludge

Working out: Turning fat into muscles

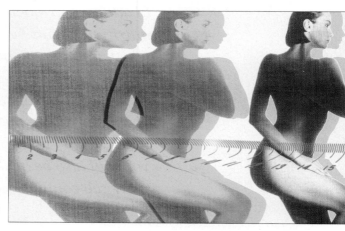

*Turbo gym: Nice upper
thighs in 4 weeks*

*In-line skating:
For firm legs*

*Foods that detoxify
and tighten the tissue*

*A power
food diet:
A good way to start*

Problem zones without problems. Not every part of the hip can be shaped to a perfect form. But you can always improve it.

WHERE DOES THE PROBLEM LIE?

Too much fat and flab at the buttocks, stomach, hips, and upper thighs. Where do these problems come from?

Problem #1: Body structure

Some people may believe that there are fixed measurements for what the natural female form should be. On the contrary: The relationship between bone structure and fat distribution can vary. And since they are inherited, which means they are set in the genes, their basic structure cannot be changed. Therefore, if you have an athletic or stocky body-type, all the diet, exercise, and creams cannot produce a willowy figure with narrow hips. But this is no reason to give up, because every woman can make the best out of what she has gotten from nature with the help of sports, nutrition, and beauty care. And this book can help you reach your optimum.

Problems #2 & #3: Connective tissue and female hormones

After the genes, which determine the form of the pelvis, the specific structure of a woman's connective tissue is the main difficulty with problem zones. In contrast to the connective tissue of a man, where the pattern is horizontal and the fibers are not anchored on the skin, a woman's fibers are anchored to the skin and divide the fat vertically to create little pouches of fat. That allows better flexibility of the tissue, which is necessary especially during pregnancy. Unfortunately, it also fosters the accumulation of fat and water. And the more female sex hormones (estrogen and progesterone) the body produces, the more of both settle. A frequent result is dimpled, cottage-cheese looking fat (see pages 14–15).

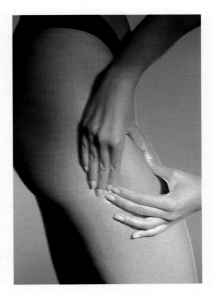

Do you have cellulite? Try the pinch test on page 17.

Problem #4: Loose muscles

If the muscles of the problem zones between the waist and knee are used too little, they sag and accumulate fat. In addition, the blood flow in the tissue worsens, which contributes to cellulite. Anyone who regularly works out enhances the tension of the muscles (muscle tone) and makes it hard for fat and water to accumulate in the tissue. In addition to that, oxygen gets into the blood through intensive sports activity, which increases the burning of fat (see pages 86–87).

Problem #5: Tissue sludge

The metabolic waste of dead cells can lodge anywhere in the body—from the organs to cells to in-between cells. Although they are constantly being carried away by the lymph, they tend to accumulate in the problem zone areas, where circulation is sluggish and tissue sludge forms. This sludge theory, however, is disputed among doctors, since even the most modern devices could not prove such accumulations so far. Alternative healers prefer to speak of this condition as high blood acidity (acidosis). That means that the body's acid-base balance is disturbed, which affects the cleansing of the connective-tissue cells. Wrong nutrition and lack of oxygen in the tissue from too little movement are considered to be the main causes for this disturbance.

Problem #6: Weight

The existence of problem zones is especially noticeable when a person is overweight. The buttocks, stomach, hips, and upper thighs are where most of the fat and cellulite accumulate. Although losing weight helps, the number of fat cells is genetically determined. Therefore, there is little you can do to change it. At the most, you can lose some of the fat in the problem zone areas. But it is difficult to keep it off when your body has been accustomed to a certain amount of body fat since infancy.

Fast weight-loss programs and crash diets are useless. Even though you lose some of the fat, your body quickly strives for its "normal condition" again as soon as some more calories are available. After a few crash diets, the body's set point lowers. This means that the point at which the body can manage well with the amount of calories available is lowered. As a result, if the body gets more energy, instead of using it up, it accumulates it in the form of fat in the fat tissue.

To escape from this vicious cycle, you need to make a long-term commitment to changing your diet. A good starting point is an anti-cellulite diet with certain "power foods" and 1200 calories a day. You will immediately see the results of a few lost pounds, which may help motivate you to continue (see page 98).

Problem #7: A good self-image

Having a good self-image is healthy and absolutely necessary when you want to get your problem zones into the best shape they can be. Being critical and objective when viewing yourself in the mirror can strengthen your discipline and perseverance at muscle training, diet, or daily massages with anti-cellulite products. But it is important to be realistic about your body and the small improvements it makes through muscle training, dieting, and body care. Having too-strict standards will only cheat you out of the success you've achieved and the realization that your body is great even when it's not perfect.

Empowering yourself: Working towards fitness and a good figure.

SMOOTHIN

CHAPTER I

G THE SKIN

The main difficulty with problem zones is cellulite. Where does the "orange-peel skin" come from? What can one do to get rid of, or at least smooth, it? Everything that you need to know about body care—baths, massages, and surgical treatments—as well as a daily planner (see pages 46–47) are in this chapter.

What products, applications, or surgical procedures are there for fighting cellulite?

Possibility #1: Anti-cellulite products

There are creams, gels, and oils that contain substance for better circulation to help reduce tissue sludge. They must be used daily and, depending on the instructions, in combination with a massage, either manual or with a device. Most reputable companies strongly recommend that you use their product in conjunction with an exercise and diet program (see page 17ff).

Possibility #2: Nature's aids

Seaweed packs, mud baths, or potato masks—anyone who prefers to use natural products can try to attack cellulite by alternative and homemade methods. (The active agents of some anti-cellulite products also come from natural ingredients.) However, making your own preparations and applications can be a lot of work as well as a lot of mess (see page 22ff).

WHAT ARE THE POSSIBILITIES?

Possibility #3: Cellulite massages

An important accompaniment to the anti-cellulite products are massages. The gentle, rhythmic pressure onto the skin tissue enhances blood flow and stimulates lymph flow. Whether you're doing the massage manually, with a roller, or with an electric device, it is important to do it regularly (see page 28ff).

Possibility #4: Hydrotherapy

People have known since the old days that water has an excellent effect on the skin tissue. Whether taking a shower or bath, or being in the sauna and steam room, the warm temperature offers great stimulation of blood flow and, thus, reduces tissue sludge. When taking a bath, you can gently massage the cellulite areas to enhance circulation. The ocean is an ideal place for a massage.

Minerals and algae in the ocean are known to have healing properties and help to dissolve cellulite (see page 30ff).

Possibility #5: Surgery

Liposuction, or lipoplasty, is a surgical procedure to remove cellulite and unwanted fat deposits from the body. This surgery is done in the problem zone areas. A small incision is made on the skin and a hollow tube is inserted underneath it to suck out the surplus fat cells from the tissue through low pressure. The scars from liposuction are small and strategically placed so that they're hard to see. Although this procedure is normally safe, like any surgery it carries a certain amount of risk (see page 35ff).

Possibility #6: Spa treatments

There are other professional, non-invasive methods to tighten and smooth out the problem zones: laser treatment, deep heating, body wraps, and so on. These professional methods are, in general, not cheap and their effectiveness is often disputed. Whichever method you choose, unless you do it with an exercise and diet program, your results will probably be limited (see page 41ff).

Possibility #7: Electric stimulation

There are passive workout methods that help in body sculpting. Their goal is to replace the exhaustive gym workouts through rhythmically activating the muscular system with electric stimulation therapy. As a result, the "orange-peel skin" will diminish because of enhanced blood supply that will increase the burning up of calories (see page 45).

ANTI-CELLULITE PRODUCTS

Anti-cellulite products are supposed to remove tissue sludge and tighten skin. But do they really work?

The cosmetics industry offers numerous products for fighting cellulite. They come in different forms. There are gels, creams, lotions, and oils. What form they come in has little bearing on their effectiveness. Rather, it is the active ingredients and carrier substances in the product that determine their success. In addition to that, cosmetics companies want to offer a "comfortable" product that requires little time and effort to use. So which product is the one for you? It is based on your personal choice and preference in regards to the product's smell, consistency, promise of effectiveness, and how it feels when applied.

■ Gels have a feeling of freshness when applied. One big advantage to a gel is that you only have to smooth it on, as opposed to massaging it in. The gel is immediately absorbed into the skin without a sticky or greasy residue. It leaves a light scent behind. There are alcohol-free anti-cellulite gels that are good for people with sensitive skin.

■ Creams generally need to be massaged into the skin in order for the ingredients to be well-absorbed. Because of this, creams are often offered in combination with a small mechanical massaging device (see also page 28). The advantage of using a massaging device is that it works the tissue and increases blood circulation.

■ Thermal creams warm up the skin so that the blood vessels beneath it become enlarged. This way, water and tissue sludge are supposed to be transported away better. Thermal creams can also cause the skin to redden. Therefore, be careful about using this product if you have spider veins or varicose veins.

■ Lotions apply smoothly. They dry quickly and are usually not greasy.

■ Oils are needed as lubricants for certain kinds of cellulite treatments, such as electrotherapy.

What's the goal of anti-cellulite products?

It is always the same. The different anti-cellulite products:

■ stimulate lymphatic circulation so that tissue sludge, excess water, and cellular wastes can be carried away and eliminated faster. (The lymphatic system is the body's own "metabolic waste disposal." The lymph—the colorless fluid that bathes the tissues and cells of the body—draws the body's wastes from the spaces between the cells and carries them to be filtered away by the lymph nodes. Lymphatic circulation is dependent upon muscle contraction and breathing.);

■ stimulate cellular activity in order to accelerate the formation of new cells and,

Upper thighs: Their shape comes from your genes; but you can do something for tighter skin.

> **PINCH TEST:**
>
> Squeeze a section of skin in your upper thigh with your thumb and index finger. Does it look like the surface of an orange? Don't worry, that is not yet cellulite but the typical structure of the female connective tissue, which becomes visible under pressure. It's only considered cellulite when the skin shows impressions and arches, like a matress, without squeezing it.

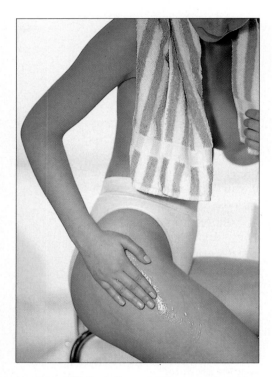

An anti-cellulite gel after a shower is quickly absorbed into the skin without needing to be massaged in.

thus, strengthen the connective tissues of the problem zone areas;

■ stimulate the metabolism of fat, especially during a diet, so that the fat cells can empty out faster in the cellulite tissue;

■ stimulate the supply of blood, because tissue that is well supplied with blood is better nourished and has better circulation. As a result, the skin looks smoother and tighter.

What active ingredients are used?

Some ingredients that are commonly used in anti-cellulite products include

extracts from ivory, horse-chestnut, arnica, fennel, birch bark, cypress, wild wine, and seaweed. Some of the more effective ingredients are:

■ Caffeine, combined with an extract from the cola nut, causes the breakdown of fat within the fat cells. This inhibits fat accumulation while accelerating its elimination by the lymph. The cola extract helps by enhancing the circulation in the tissue.

■ Theophylline, which comes from tea leaves, increases the blood flow in the very fine blood vessels and eliminates excess water from the tissue.

■ Butcher's broom (Latin name: *Ruscus acuelatus*) helps strengthen the walls of the blood vessels. It also aids in the elimination of tissue sludge and cellular waste by the lymph.

■ Guarana comes from the seeds of the Brazilian Guaran shrub. It is said to enhance the basal metabolism of the cells and to further the emission of catecholamine, which is the hormone group that is supposed to accelerate the reduction of fat in the cells (especially during a diet).

■ Ginkgo is an active agent that comes from the Asian *Ginkgo biloba* tree and is used mostly in combination with caffeine. It is supposed to improve the body's circulation and help decrease fat.

■ Gotu kola (Latin name: *Centella asiatica*), a tropical climbing plant, supplies the extract *Acidum asiaticum*, which improves blood flow.

■ Silicon is a mineral that is necessary for the formation of collagen for connective tissue. It also promotes healthy nails and hair. It is supposed to improve the elasticity of the tissue fibers. (Silicon works better when eaten from food sources rather than applied topically.)

■ Hydroxy acid, which belongs to the AHAs (alpha hydroxy acids) and is a fruit acid, accelerates the natural peeling off process of the skin. As a result, it is supposed to stimulate the formation of new cells, and the new layer of skin is more ready to absorb anti-cellulite active ingredients.

■ Nicotin acid produces the warming effect in the thermal creams.

How can you find out the active ingredients of a product?

The main active ingredients (although not usually the carrier substances) are, in most cases, listed on the packaging box and/or the product itself. The quantity is listed in descending order. That means, the active ingredient with the highest concentration is mentioned first.

WHAT TO DO FOR STRETCH MARKS?

Even though stretch marks (striae) at the hips, stomach, and upper thighs do not have anything directly to do with cellulite, you can treat them as you are working on your cellulite. Stretch marks are believed to be a kind of scar in the connective tissue, which comes from overstretching the elastin and collagen fibers. They are caused by mechanical stress and hormonal changes within the body. They frequently occur during puberty, after pregnancy, after hormonal therapy, and as a result of extreme weight gain. Unfortunately, pale stretch marks cannot be removed. But by regularly massaging the area (either manually or with a suitable massaging device; see page 28), the width and depth of the stretch marks can decrease in time. The pink or yellowish-white discolorations can also become paler. Special compounds made up of the effective agents seaweed-silicon and hydroxiprolin are helpful. You can alternate using them with your anti-cellulite product if you happen to have both cellulite and stretch marks in the same area.

Is there proof of the effectiveness of the products?

A good cosmetic product does not make its way into the hands of the consumer without being first tested many times by the manufacturer. This applies to anti-cellulite products as well. They are tested not only in vitro (in an artificial environment, such as a test tube) but also in vivo (on the skin of voluntary test persons). Consumer testing, in collaboration with doctors, is the most simple "proof" of the effectiveness of a new product—even though it is also the most inaccurate one. Too many subjective predilections of the users, such as the consistency of the product (cream, gel, or oil), its smell, or the way it feels on the skin, influence the results, which make objective statements about the actual effectiveness on the tissue almost impossible. Measurements with instruments that were developed specifically for skin tests are more objective and precise. These tests are generally done before the application of the product and 4 weeks afterwards.

■ <u>Sonography (ultrasound)</u> helps prove the removal of tissue sludge. The highly sensitive ultrasound waves make a two-dimensional depiction of the skin possible. Through this, the fat tissue can be clearly distinguished from the muscle tissue and a decrease of the fat volume can be documented after the treatment.

A similar procedure is through the measurement of fat volume with the use of infrared rays.

Cellulite control: Measuring yourself once a week is better than weighing yourself every day (see page 99).

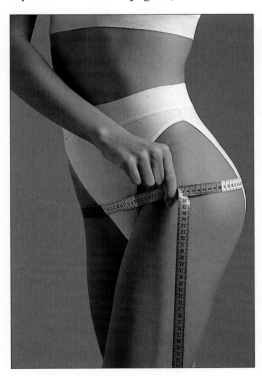

■ <u>The nuclear spin tomography</u> is a medical diagnosis procedure that is also used for the measurement of fat tissue. The resonance of the electrowaves in the different tissue layers is transformed into three-dimensional images that can be evaluated.

■ <u>Thermography</u> makes visible any improvement in blood supply. Skin temperature is measured by foils with liquid crystals that change their color when the temperature changes. Zones which are poorly supplied with blood are colder and show a brown color, while warm, well-supplied areas look blue.

■ A firmometer and twistometer measure the skin's elasticity. The firmometer puts pressure onto the skin and the twistometer slightly twists it. The more elastic the skin is, the faster it returns to its original position.

What results can you realistically expect?

Research results presented by the manufacturers of products are usually gotten in a respectable and reliable manner. Nevertheless, experts agree that improving a cellulite area depends not only on using a good product, but also on having a certain discipline. That means:

■ The cosmetic improvement of anti-cellulite products on the skin's surface is undisputed, because almost all the products also contain skin-caring ingredients and substances that provide the skin with moisture.

■ The products must be used daily (or according to the instructions of the manufacturer).

■ Perseverance is necessary for a lasting effect. Stopping or performing the regiment

WHY CAN SLIM WOMEN ALSO HAVE CELLULITE?

Because of the structure of their connective tissue, women tend to hold fat (see page 9) regardless whether they are slim or heavy. During pregnancy and hormonal therapy, these tissues can become visible. In addition to that, everything that impedes the elimination of waste in the body furthers the formation of cellulite: Lymph blockage, slow digestion, poor blood circulation, or bad liver, bladder, and kidney functions. Also, too much stress, too little sleep, too much consumption of alcohol, but especially heavy smoking can further cellulite formation in slim women.

inconsistently may risk losing what results that have already been achieved.

■ Using the right products while actively taking care of your skin with massages + sports activities + correct nutrition (calorie reduction) is needed in order to attack the problem. An improvement in problem zone areas occurs only when blood supply is increased through massages and water applications (see p. 30), when the

tension in the muscular system increases, and when a clear decrease in fat is visible (through dieting).

How often should you apply anti-cellulite products?

It is best to use them daily. Even better would be to use them in the morning and evening. Most manufacturers recommend using their products after taking a shower and after a massage (for example, with a brush or loofah glove). Gels and lotions only need to be spread onto the skin while creams and oils should be applied when getting a massage. Thereby, it is less important how much gel or cream you apply but that you use them conscientiously and regularly. An occasional application will not produce any kind of noticeable effect. You need to be consistent in your application in order for any long-term results to be seen on your skin. This may even have ramifications into your other disciplines. Being dedicated to taking care of your skin can give you the determination to successfully stick to your physical activities and diet.

Hip area: Slimmer from dieting, tighter from sports, smoother from massage and anti-cellulite products.

NATURE'S AIDS

If you don't mind the inconvenience, you can also attack cellulite with homemade products and remedies.

Commercial anti-cellulite products contain a mixture of natural ingredients. Using these commercial products is simple, hygienic, and time-saving. Homemade natural products, which are said to have a cellulite-improving effect, are a lot more cumbersome. They can take some time to prepare and apply, and they can also be very messy to use. In regards to their effect, you can see improvements if you apply them regularly in combination with intensive muscle-training and good nutrition.

RECIPE FOR ROSE SALT-BATH ADDITIVE

Alternately layer 2 pounds of coarse sea salt with fresh, strong-smelling rose leaves in a large preserve jar. After about 3 weeks, the salt will have absorbed the rose fragrances so that you can use it as a bath additive. Using table salt as a substitute for sea salt will not work, because 80% of table salt is sodium chloride. The minerals that are needed are missing if you use table salt.

Seaweed, with its high-mineral content, is especially effective in fighting cellulite.

Natural product #1: Sea salt

A favorite among the natural products is sea salt from the Dead Sea (sold in pharmacies and natural beauty stores). Sea salt from the Dead Sea has some ingredients that are also in table salt, but it contains more magnesium, potassium, iron, and iodine. Magnesium has a strong stimulating effect on the skin's metabolism. Sea salt draws out excess water from the tissue without drying it out.

■ The most comfortable way to enjoy its effect is to take a long bath once or twice a week. To do that, dissolve a pound of coarse salt-crystals (from the pharmacy, health-food store, natural store) in hot water and pour it into the bathtub. Ideally, the bathwater should be around your body temperature (98.6°F/37°C). Bathe for about 15 minutes and shower briefly to rinse off the salt. Then wrap yourself in a robe and rest for 30 minutes. Using cream is unnecessary because the water, which remains on the skin's surface, does not simply evaporate, but is bound on the skin through the salt and acid. (Recipe for an aromatic sea-salt rose bath in box.)

■ Another way to use sea salt is exfoliating with coarse salt crystals and olive oil. As a result, the skin is not only perfectly supplied with blood, but it is also freed from dead surface cells so that it feels smoother and more tender afterwards. (See recipe on page 25.)

■ In order to enhance the effect, you can also drink specially prepared seawater (available in pharmacies and health-food stores). It helps to eliminate tissue sludge and aid digestion. Try drinking a large glass every day. The seawater is diluted with

Good for the body and soul: Bathing with homemade rose salt. See recipe box on this page.

normal water at a ratio of 1:3. There is no danger of taking too much salt. Two rolls of bread contain about as much salt as your daily glass of seawater.

Natural product #2: Seaweed

Wraps with mud, moor mud, or wheat grass tighten and detoxify cellulite tissue.

Two pounds of seaweed contain all the active substances in about 26,000 gallons of seawater. Green, brown, or red seaweed plants are considered an especially potent cellulite remedy. The high content of mineral salts, trace elements, amino acids, and vitamins specifically speeds up the fat metabolism in the tissue so that, in combination with a good diet, there is a faster reduction of fat accumulation and tissue sludge. Seaweed also stimulates the liver, which is the most important detoxifying organ in the body, to filter excess estrogen from the blood. (Estrogen is the female hormone that is, to a great degree, responsible for the way cellulite looks.)

The best time to begin a 6-week long intensive treatment with seaweed is shortly after menstruation, because then the estrogen level has returned to its normal level.

■ Every 2 days, take a bath in the morning or evening with liquid seaweed extracts (available in pharmacies and health-food stores). The water should not be warmer than 102°F/39°C. Do not bathe for longer than 30 minutes. Afterwards, massage an anti-cellulite product that also contains seaweed extracts on the problem zone areas.

■ In addition, drink a cup of seaweed tea (available in pharmacies and health-food stores) half an hour before your main meals. If you don't like the taste, take seaweed capsules instead.

■ You can easily make an anti-cellulite pack from Agar Agar, a powder that comes from red seaweed (available in health-food stores). Mix twenty drops camphor oil and two egg yolks into a paste; its effect lasts for 15

MASSAGE FIRST, THEN WRAP

Body packs and wraps work better if you massage the area of the problem zone beforehand for several minutes with a cellulite roller, body brush, or loofah glove. This will increase the circulation of the skin area so that when the pores open up, the active ingredients can penetrate better.

minutes. Afterwards, shower it off with lukewarm water.

Natural product #3: Wheat grass

As opposed to what its name suggests, wheat grass is not simply a grain but a salt-water plant as well. It contains a high concentration of sixteen vitamins plus an abundant supply of calcium, magnesium, and iron.

■ Mix the powder (available in health-food stores) with water to form a paste so that you can apply it on the problem zone areas. After 20 minutes, wash it off in the shower.

■ Wheat grass is also available in the form of capsules so that you can ingest it and treat your skin from the inside.

Natural product #4: Mud

Mud is considered part of the healing earth. Moor mud or mud from the Dead Sea is rich in minerals, which are said to have, among other things, an anti-cellulite effect.

■ Mud is available as a powder (available in pharmacies, health-food stores, and natural-food stores). Mix it with warm water and chamomile tea and then apply it with a soft brush as a thick paste onto the cellulite parts. When it dries, the covered skin warms up so that the blood supply increases. After 15–20 minutes, soften the mud under the shower so that you can rinse it off.

■ You can also <u>drink</u> specially prepared blends of moor mud and healing earth products. Like the seaweed drink, you might need some time to get used to it. But they are suppose to remove acids and tissue sludge. Each day dissolve a teaspoon of mud powder in a glass of water or apple juice.

Natural product #5: Aromatherapy oil

Aromatherapy oils are absorbed through the nose and skin. The fragrance molecules not only influence mood, but they

A sea salt rub makes the skin wonderfully smooth (see recipe in box on this page).

---

also activate the metabolism in the connective tissue. Of course this depends on the correct blend.

■ Mix 30 ml jojoba or wheat germ oil (available in pharmacies) with ten drops of grapefruit oil and five drops each of rosemary oil and cypress oil as your base. Then massage this anti-cellulite mixture in a circular motion from bottom to top into the skin of the problem zone. Tightly wrap thin self-adhesive plastic wrapping around it. Under the wrapping, the skin warms up and the oils are better absorbed. Rest for 45 minutes warmly wrapped under a blanket. Using an infrared lamp, if you have one, can increase the effect of oil and wrapping.

■ Recipe for a <u>tightening compress</u>: Boil about 2 cups (½ liter) of water and then let

---

it cool. Mix fifteen drops of rosemary oil or, as a substitute, horsechestnut, with half a cup of condensed milk, and stir it into the water. Dip a wide mull bandage into the water, wring it out, and wrap it as tightly as possible around the stomach, hips, and/or upper thigh area. If needed, wrap self-adhesive plastic wrapping over it as well.

Important: When you buy aromatherapy oils, make sure that they are really massage oils rather than for scenting rooms. Do not buy too much oil. Mix only one week's supply each time, since the pure plant oil can become rancid quickly.

Natural product #6: Herb teas and herbal wraps

■ Birch leaf tea can help eliminate excess water. Add three pinches per cup and let it sit for 10 minutes. Drink one cup in the morning, afternoon, and evening, before eating.

■ To make an herbal wrap, pour a handful each of dried ivory and greater celandine (available from herb stores) into a quart (liter) of boiling water. Cover the pot and let it cook for 15 minutes. Dip cloths into it and wrap them as warm as you can tolerate around your hips, stomach, and upper thighs. Stay well wrapped under a blanket until the compresses have cooled off.

ANTI-CELLULITE MASSAGES

A daily massage is the most important thing to do if you want to get rid of cellulite. But should you do it manually or with a device?

Anti-cellulite compounds are more effective when combined with a massage. Why? Because the gentle pressure from the hands or a massaging device will accelerate the "cleansing" of the tissue via the lymphs. This colorless fluid, which circulates through a vast network of small capillaries called lymphatics, is often blocked, in the case of cellulite, by an excess of fat cells. As a result, excess fluid and waste products from cell metabolism cannot be completely drawn out and eliminated. They literally become blocked in the connective tissue to form the dents seen in cellulite.

By the way, each massage is more effective when you apply an anti-cellulite compound beforehand.

Manual massage

In a manual massage, you roll and tug the problem zone area with your bare hands. This is considered to be a deep and especially effective method. You can adjust the pressure and strength of the massage according to your liking and, depending on your sensitivity, you can work more on

A massage roller must feel pleasant on the skin and be comfortably gripped so that you can do it for 10 minutes each day.

> ## WATCH OUT FOR VARICOSE VEINS!
>
> **Do not massage (either manually or with a device) areas in which there are varicose veins, spider veins (couperose skin), or are in danger of forming blood clots (thrombosis). If you have any of these problems, or are uncertain if massaging will cause these conditions, consult a specialist before you begin.**

the skin surface or deeper into the tissue.

■ Rolling the skin involves pressing together a piece of skin with the thumb and forefinger of both hands and then pushing it less than a half inch (1 centimeter) upwards. Drag the fingers to the next section of skin, grab hold of it, and knead the entire surface that way, little by little, from the knees upwards to the hip.

■ A tugging massage is simpler. Gently lift the skin with your fingertips a half inch by a half inch. Lay your palm on the skin surface and

bend your fingers so that the tips tug the skin and press it slightly together. Then bring the skin briefly upward without pulling. It is best to tug with short fingernails; otherwise you can bruise the skin.

Skin brushing

A daily massage with a not too hard body brush, or a horsehair, sisal, loofah, or woven glove made of synthetic fibers, can increase blood supply and smooth out the skin surface. An increased blood supply can prevent the buildup of waste and lymph blockage, while the daily removal of dead surface cells from brushing makes the skin increasingly more tender. The brushing will not get rid of the "orange-peel skin" look, but it will make your skin become more permeable to the active ingredients of anti-cellulite compounds.

All skin brushes and gloves can be used dry or wet. It is best to brush in small circles, but do not press too hard. Your skin should not burn or get scratched up afterwards. Always massage towards the heart.

For instance, if you're working the right leg, massage from the knee upward. Work a little harder on the spots where there's a higher concentration of cellulite.

Cellulite rollers

Cosmetic companies offer a number of cellulite rollers for the problem zone areas. This system of burls, rolls, balls, or lamellas feels gentle but it has a long-lasting effect on the tissue being worked on.

You can buy these rollers separately or as a package with the anti-cellulite product. Buying one of these "combination packs" makes sense, especially if the massage roller has harder edges. If you do not apply cream beforehand, it can damage the tissue as well as feel uncomfortable. Follow the instructions before you begin using the roller. They will tell you whether you should use the roller before or after applying cream, how much pressure to apply when using it, and if you should massage in a circular or upward motion. These factors can help determine the success of the treatment. Before you buy a cellulite roller, you should carefully test how it feels on your skin and make sure you can comfortably grip it, because you should use it for at least 10 minutes each day; 20 minutes would be optimal.

Electric devices

Electrical massaging devices require less force and strain to use. Therefore, you might use them longer and get better results. But, as a general rule, you should not expect these electrical devices to be more effective than the manual cellulite rollers. These electrical massaging devices are modeled after the ones used in beauty treatment centers and health spas. The goal is to remove tissue sludge and stimulate blood circulation in order to further decrease the amount

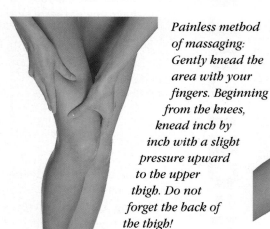

Painless method of massaging: Gently knead the area with your fingers. Beginning from the knees, knead inch by inch with a slight pressure upward to the upper thigh. Do not forget the back of the thigh!

of fat already reduced from a diet. Your skin sensitivity, again, should determine which electric device is good for you. Some electrical massaging devices can be expensive.

The most common electric devices are:

■ Massager with kneading effect: Two pairs of conical massage burls turn in opposite directions. The kneading feeling is compara-

ble to that of an intensive hand massage.

■ Pressure turning massager: Nine concentrically-arranged burls pulsate in a wave shape at two different speed levels.

■ Gliding wave massager: Two rollers, which are turned towards each other, lift the skin slightly and shift it like waves.

■ Vacuum massager: Based on Endermologie therapy used in spas, a vacuum tube is moved slowly back and forth over the skin. It gently lifts and kneads the skin in a

rhythmic motion. The skin must be oiled beforehand so that the device can easily glide over it.

Daily massage with a body brush:
Prevents cellulite formation and makes the skin smooth as silk.

Massaging with loofah gloves: Accelerates blood supply.

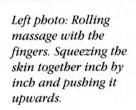

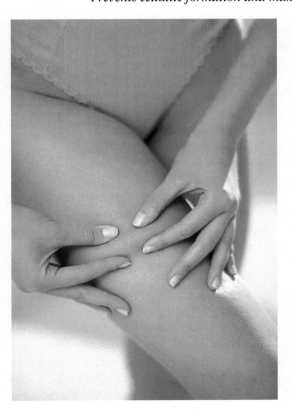

Left photo: Rolling massage with the fingers. Squeezing the skin together inch by inch and pushing it upwards.

Right photo: Cellulite massage with an electrical massaging device is the easiest alternative.

Water transports active agents onto the skin, offers gentle pressure massage, and invigorates the body with its warm temperature.

HYDROTHERAPY

Hydrotherapy #1: Bath

Taking baths or showers can help tighten the skin of the problem zone areas. But keep in mind that you cannot expect wonders from simply bathing. You should view hydrotherapy baths as one part of a comprehensive anti-cellulite program.

Recommended for cellulite: Hydrotherapy baths with active substances from thermal springs.

Bath and shower additives in anti-cellulite products contain active substances from thermal springs with essential minerals and trace elements (potassium- and sodium-chloride, copper, magnesium, manganese, zinc, and iron), which nourish the skin and body. As in the case with the anti-cellulite products, extracts from seaweeds, horsetail, ivory, horse-chestnut, rosemary, and sage are often used in these bath and shower additives. The active agents are usually channeled into the skin with the help of liposomes, which aid in enhancing the effect.

You can also make hydrotherapy bath additives from aromatherapy oils or herbs. Here are two recipes for such bath mixtures:

■ Mix six drops of juniper oil and two drops each of aromatherapy oil from orange, cypress, and lemon.

■ Mix 3½ ounces (100 grams) of dried blackberry leaves with one cup of honey and twenty drops of lavender oil.

Important: Avoid high temperatures when bathing. Although hot water increases blood supply, it will also expand the connective tissues, which is not good because it will allow for more pockets of cellulite. The bathwater should not be more than 97°F/36°C, and you should not bathe longer than 30 minutes. After bathing, shower with cool water, dab the skin only slightly dry, and then try to build up a sweat by being well-covered in bed.

Hydrotherapy #2: Alternating warm and cool shower

Alternating between a warm and cool shower allows a quick change of temperature. The warm water expands the blood vessels, the cool water contracts them. This switching improves the elasticity, which affects the tightening of problem zone areas. In addition, it enhances the blood supply of even the finest capillary vessels so that the tissue is better supplied with nutrients and detoxified more thoroughly. If done daily, this method can be an effective contribution to the tightening and smoothing of cellulite parts.

Do not go from too extreme temperatures—e.g., from very hot to very cold—since it may be too much for blood vessels and tissues. Moderately cool water in alternation with warm water has proven to be better for weak connective tissues, especially if

Cold water shooting from a strong jet is a way of preventing cellulite. If you have soft connective tissue, make the water cool and lessen the pressure.

these areas contain expanded small veins (spider veins).

■ <u>What to do</u>: After cleaning your body with warm water, rinse off the problem zones with cool water for at least a minute. Then turn the water warm again for 2 minutes before finally showering with cool water. You can alternate between warm and cool as often as you like, but always work the areas beginning from your feet upwards. Finish with a cool jet rinse, and then firmly rub your body dry using a not too fluffy towel; that will give your blood supply another push. Since your skin is now especially ready to absorb active agents, massage an

Keeping your legs on level with your body during a steambath and/or sauna improves blood and lymph flow.

Applying ice or a cold pack stimulates the blood supply and prevents cellulite from forming.

anti-cellulite compound onto the problem zones in circular motions.

**Hydrotherapy #3:
Rubbing with ice**

Ice stimulates the skin's blood supply even more than cold water. Therefore, daily ice massages can contribute to the tightening of skin in the problem zone areas.

■ A <u>cold pack</u> from a pharmacy, which can also be used as a first aid, is the easiest to handle. Put the transparent bag with its blue contents in the freezer and then work over the skin in

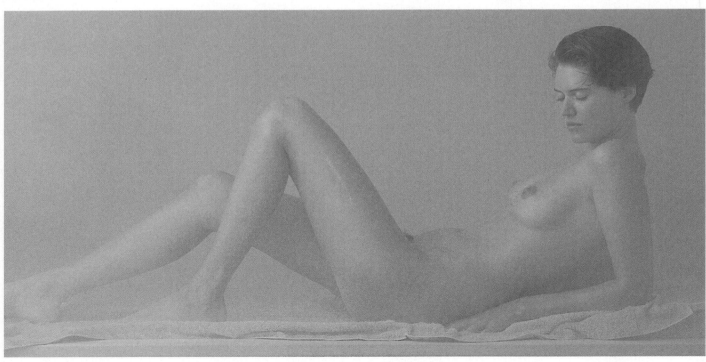

fast strokes after a shower (but before applying an anti-cellulite compound).

■ <u>Cold sheet wraps</u> are a little more cumbersome. For this you need two wide strips of plastic foil (cut out from garbage bags, if you don't have any). Cool them in ice water or in a freezer and then wrap them tightly around the upper thighs. Put a big terry-

Rubs with vinegar water refresh and help keep the skin tight.

cloth towel over them, and lie down in bed with a hot water bottle or a heating pad for an hour. In about 5 minutes, the skin will begin to perspire. Cold sheet wraps can help drain the tissue only

in combination with a diet. Only using cold sheet wraps will not help. This is similar to cold treatments done in spas.

Hydrotherapy #4: Rubs with vinegar water

Diluted fruit vinegar helps keep the skin tight and can be used easily each day after taking a shower. You need 100 ml of fruit vinegar mixed with 30 ml of 96% alcohol (available at the pharmacy) as well as with ten drops thyme or myrrh oil (aromatherapy oil). Put the vinegar mix in a bottle, shake well, and store it in the refrigerator. This is enough for about ten applications. It is important to use fruit vinegar, because it contains mineral substances that stimulate circulation and blood supply. The thyme and myrrh aromatherapy oils have, in addition, a balancing effect on the body's metabolism and inner organs.

■ <u>What to do</u>: Stand in the bathtub or shower stall. Pour the vinegar mix into the palm of your hand and soak it up with a large natural sponge. Rub your entire body, beginning at your feet, continuing up the legs, and finally stroking the upper body and arms. Your skin should feel wonderful. Unless you have extremely dry skin, you can skip applying body lotion afterwards.

Hydrotherapy #5: Sauna and steambath

It is not possible to become slim from simply sweating it out in the sauna. The water in your body that is lost is immediately replenished by subsequently drinking more water, which is absolutely necessary. Nevertheless, detoxifying your body with saunas or steambaths is an important part of every cellulite treatment. The repeated alternation of warm and cold has a positive effect on the cellulite tissue—just like taking showers with alternately warm and cool water. This improves the elasticity of the blood vessels and strengthens the blood supply, which improves metabolism in the tissue and enhances elimination of salt and other toxins via the pores.

If you have cellulite, and especially if you have spider veins, sit only on the lower or middle bench in the sauna. It is important that you keep your legs level with your body. When you let them hang, blockages can occur, which is detrimental in the case of cellulite and especially varicose and spider veins. When you shower afterwards, do not have the water shoot out too strongly. The best way to treat cellulite is with gentle streams of water coming from adjustable showerheads or water buckets.

The contouring of problem zone areas can be done with the help of the most up-to-date surgical procedures and instruments.

SURGERY

The problem zone areas that are resistant to exercise, diet, and anti-cellulite products may require surgery.

Have you really tried everything you could to get rid of the dents and ugly bulges from cellulite on your upper thighs for at least 6 months? Including intensive sports and daily workouts? Using anti-cellulite products, daily massages, saunas/steambaths, and cool water? Have you changed your diet to "power foods?" If after all this your skin, especially around the area of your hips, buttocks, and upper thighs, does not meet your expectations, then you can either:

■ Accept your body the way it is now, based on its genetic disposition and your physical development, and continue to keep it in the best shape it can be, or

■ Opt for plastic surgery to contour the problem zones to the way you wish them to be.

Wrong reason: Choosing surgery as an easy method

If you believe that you can save yourself time and effort by having plastic surgery, you are terribly wrong. You can achieve the optimal and longest-lasting results of an operation only if your skin and tissue are in the best condition beforehand. Also, plastic surgery is no guarantee that your money will be well spent. In other words, you should not view plastic surgery as an alternative to a healthy diet, muscle training, and vigorous skin-care treatment. You still need to do all those things when working on your problem zones.

The right method and doctor

Here are three kinds of surgery to consider when it comes to smoothing out and contouring the problem zones:

■ Liposuction, which is also known as suction-assisted lipectomy, lipoplasty, fat suction, or suction lipectomy, is a body-sculpting technique that most people have heard of.

■ Celluloliolysis and/or electrolipolysis

■ Ultrasonic-assisted liposuction

All three methods can only be done by plastic surgeons who specialize in their respective techniques. Sometimes you need to visit and interview several to find one that you are comfortable with.

Method #1: Liposuction

This is a surgical procedure to remove unwanted fat deposits, which you would not be able to get rid of through dieting or exercising, from specific areas of the body. Remember that liposuction is not a substitute for weight reduction. Although liposuction can distinctly reshape the basic silhouette of your

Many women dream of wearing tight-fitting clothes that flatter their figure. Plastic surgery may be the answer.

body, it cannot smooth out the unevenly textured skin from cellulite. To consider this procedure, you should have firm, elastic skin, because that will ensure a better final contour. Hanging skin will not reshape to your body's new silhouette. It may need to be removed surgically, which will leave visible scars behind.

■ How is the procedure done? Only minimal incisions, which are later hardly visible, are necessary. The incisions are large enough so that a hollow tube, called a cannula, can be inserted. A machine that creates a strong vacuum is attached to the other end of the cannula. The plastic surgeon manipulates the cannula like a fan crosswise deep within the fat layers under the skin. This way, the fat cells are broken up and suctioned out via the cannula. If you've had local anesthesia, you'll feel some vibration and friction during the procedure. You might also feel a slight stinging sensation if the cannula moves close to a muscle. You'll be given fluid intravenously to replace the fluid lost with the fat during the procedure. You may also be given before the procedure an injection of potassium chloride and adrenaline solution, which reduces the amount of blood loss during the liposuction and the amount of swelling afterwards. This solution also puffs up the tissue temporarily so that the plastic surgeon can see the area to be worked on better and, therefore, work more precisely. If the liposuction is extensive, you may need to have blood drawn out ahead of time in order to replace the amount lost during the procedure.

■ How will you feel? People usually feel depressed after the procedure. If you do, remember that this is normal and the depression will go away when you start to look and feel better. You may feel heavier immediately after the procedure because of the extra fluid given to you during the liposuction. The suctioned areas will be bruised and swollen. You may also feel a burning sensation as well as stiffness and soreness in those areas. If

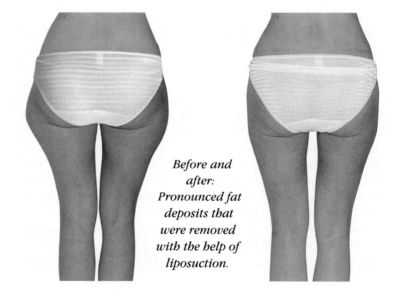

Before and after: Pronounced fat deposits that were removed with the help of liposuction.

needed, your plastic surgeon may prescribe some pain killers for any discomfort. There could be some bleeding, but that and any swelling should subside after 3 weeks.

■ What can you expect? Your stitches will probably be removed 5–10 days after the procedure, and you should be back to work in 2–3 days. In general, most of

the swelling and discoloration will disappear in 1–2 months. Some may remain for as long as 6 months, or maybe longer. You should avoid any strenuous activity for 2–4 weeks, or however long your surgeon recommends. The fat deposits that were suctioned off are now gone, but you should remember that you can still gain weight again. The additional weight may not collect at the problem zone areas like before, but it can

be distributed overall in your body. If possible, you should avoid gaining more than 6–7 pounds.

■ How long does the process take? First you need to be examined, as is the case for any kind of surgery. The length of the surgery and stay afterwards depends upon the extent of the procedure. More extensive surgery may require you to stay in the hospital for 2–5 days. The bandages are removed after 4–6 days. Then you must wear an elastic bodice pants or an elastic bodice suit for at least 2 weeks. This will help your skin shrink to its new silhouette. During this time, any strenuous activity is forbidden, to avoid bleeding.

■ How much does the procedure cost? The cost varies, depending upon the area of the body being operated on, the doctor, location, and difficulty of the specific case. In general, the price ranges from $1500 to $4000. The price usually does not include pre-examination, anesthesia, hospital stay, and any additional care afterwards.

Method #2: Cellulolipolysis and/or electrolypolysis

This method is not an operation in the more restrictive sense of the word, but rather an electrotherapy treatment that literally goes beneath the skin. The technique is used when cellulite and fat deposits are limited to smaller areas. It helps smooth out the skin and get rid of the "orange-peel skin." It also somewhat reduces the circumference of hips, stomach, and upper thighs.

■ How is the procedure done? The doctor pushes several 6-inch (15-cm) long, extremely thin one-way electrodes, which are parallel to

QUESTIONS TO ASK THE PLASTIC SURGEON

Here are some questions that you should ask the plastic surgeon before he or she does any procedure on you:
■ Are you a full-time or part-time plastic surgeon?
■ Which technique and/or method do you recommend for me?
■ How often do you perform this procedure in a month or year? How many times have you done it?
■ What is the process of this procedure? What are the risks and how high is the probability of each risk?
■ Can you show me some "before and after" photos of people who have undergone the procedure that I will undergo?
■ How is the facility/hospital technically equipped and how well-trained are the staff?
■ Can I talk to previous patients who have already undergone this procedure?
■ What is the cost of the procedure? How much does the hospital stay, if needed, cost? What other additional costs are there?
■ Who will take care of the post-operative costs?
■ Who is liable if the outcome of the procedure is not what was promised?

each other, underneath the skin surface, at the cellulite areas. (For upper thigh, it is usually sixteen electrodes.) You will feel only a slight prick with each insertion. Every electrotherapy needle is connected to a machine that controls the intensity of the current, the tension, and the electrical resistance. This treatment is supposed to eliminate excess water from the fat cells. It does not, however, actually reduce fat.

■ What can you expect? The "orange-peel skin" becomes smoother, the tissue becomes tighter, and the circumference of hips, stomach, and upper thighs can be reduced by 2 inches or more. The result can last for some months—longer if you also maintain your weight and exercise to tighten the muscles.

■ What are the drawbacks? This procedure has small risks. Bruises can occur when a vessel is injured by a needle. It can hurt when the doctor hits the nerve of a skin. If you have metabolism problems, high blood pressure, or varicose veins, you should not use the cellulolypolysis treatment.

■ How long does the process take? The needles have to be inserted six to eight times in the interval of a week. Each session lasts about an hour. Before starting the treatment, extensive blood and urine examinations have to the done in order to determine the salt-water relationship of the body. Too much water can worsen the effect of the current.

■ How much does the procedure cost? Prices vary. Depending upon where you go, it could from $150 to $200 per session.

Method #3: Ultrasonic-assisted liposuction

This method, which has been practiced in Europe for several years, has recently begun to attract attention in the United States. As a method of liposuction, ultrasonic-assisted liposuction fractionates the fat cells with ultrasonic energy before removing them from the tissue. As a result, this causes almost no damage to the blood vessels and connective tissues. This method is therefore especially good for someone who has strong cellulite but very weak connective tissues.

Disadvantages: Ultrasonic-assisted liposuction cannot work very closely beneath the skin surface. Therefore, the skin adapts only to a limited extent to the decreased tissue circumference. This method produces the best results as long as the tissue is still relatively elastic. Also, local fat deposits on the outer thighs or little bulges at the stomach cannot be removed optimally with this method.

HOW DO YOU FIND THE RIGHT PLASTIC SURGEON?

In order to find a trustworthy plastic surgeon, you should first ask your friends and acquaintances if they know of one. You can also inquire at a reputable hospital or ask your family physician for the name of a good plastic surgeon. The next step is to ask for documents containing information about the procedure and prices. Once you've compiled your list of names, you should have a consultation with each plastic surgeon at the hospital or at their office. Ask them questions (see box on page 37) to get an impression of their personality. Ask the plastic surgeon for photograph documents of operation results; these will give you the best indication of their work. Make sure that the before-and-after photographs were really done by the respective surgeon. And be aware of photos that are doctored by computers. By the way, some plastic surgeons can arrange for you to talk to some of their previous patients on whom they have performed the same procedure.

At most, it can give you a rough correction of the silhouette of the body through enhanced suctioning in the respective spots.

■ How is the procedure done? The surgeon inserts a titanium probe, which is .16 inches (4 mm) thick, through a tiny cut in the skin beneath the fat tissue. The probe is connected to a hand piece that leads to an ultrasonic generator, which converts electric energy to ultrasonic energy. The high-frequency vibration bursts the fat cells that it comes in contact with. The fractionated fat and parts of the destroyed cells are then removed with a low-volume suction that is inserted parallel into the tissue. If contouring is done at the same time, more ultrasonic energy needs to be "shot" at the spots in question.

■ What can you expect? Areas treated with ultrasonic-assisted liposuction have generally smooth skin and show no traces of cellulite. Since the fat cells have been destroyed, there is normally no new formation of fat deposits in the area. But this is not the case for the adjacent areas. Here, "orange-peel skin" can form, just like before, if the tissue is not kept in shape through exercise training, massage, correct nutrition, and the other ways previously mentioned.

■ What are the drawbacks? Since all the fat cells are not

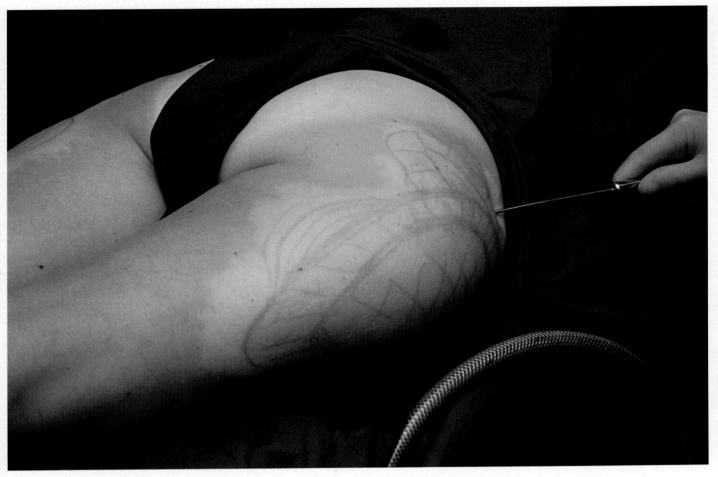

removed from the tissue completely, the remaining cells, which still have intact cell cores, can regenerate again to form complete fat cells. Also, the tissue can be overheated by the ultrasonic probe. As a result, there can be some swelling that can last for a long time (sometimes longer than 6 months). Bruises and short-term swelling, however, are normal. In this case, special massages, such as manual lymphatic drainage, can help ease the blockage in the tissue.

■ How long does the process take? First you need to be examined, as is the case for any kind of procedure. The procedure itself usually requires a stay of 24 hours in the hospital. In case of extensive work, including contouring, the stay might be longer. Tight bandages are then wrapped around the treated area for 4–7 days. After that, you must wear support stockings for

Suctioning out fat with liposuction. Before the operation, the tissue is marked and injected with a potassium-chloride solution.

at least 4 weeks. Depending on what part of the body the procedure was done on, you may have to wear an elastic bodice suit as well.

■ How much does the procedure cost? Prices vary according to surgeon and location. It could range from $3900–$4500 with hospital stay included. With contouring, it could be from $5600–$6000. Pre-examinations are additional.

SPA TREATMENTS

From herbal wraps to deep-heat therapy, spas offer special treatments for cellulite.

Anyone who wants to successfully treat cellulite cannot rely solely on one method; you need a combination of various approaches, which must include some form of muscle/exercise training, correct nutrition, and anti-cellulite products. To hope for a permanent results by only going for professional spa treatment is wrong, unless the spa offers a comprehensive cellulite program that includes diet and workouts. Participating in such a program may give you the decisive motivation kick you might need.

Spa treatment #1: Manual lymphatic drainage

A large amount of cellulite is usually linked with a slowing down of lymph flow. Lymphatic circulation relies on muscular contraction. Lack of movement causes bad circulation, which results in a stagnation of lymph. It becomes blocked in the tissue and the tissue swells up. Manual lymphatic drainage is aimed at stimulating the flow of lymph back to its normal level so that excess water and cellular waste can be expelled. The technique involves massaging in gentle, rhyth-

Color-light therapy: Wavelengths of violet light penetrate the fat tissue beneath the skin.

mic, and pumping movements along the lymph path in the direction of the lymphatic ganglions. If you have an infection, fever, or a tendency to get thrombosis, you should not have this kind of massage. It is important that the esthetician you are using has been trained from the Dr. Vodder School (from the teachings of Drs. Emil and Estrid Vodder, the physical therapists who established this method). Don't be shy to ask to see a diploma.

A treatment lasts an hour. If you have pronounced cellulite with large areas of water retention, you should massage two to three times a week for 2 months. Afterwards, one massage a month is usually sufficient. The price of a session is approximately $65, depending upon on the spa and location.

Spa treatment #2: Anti-cellulite massage

This special massage is aimed at working off the fat tissues that are beneath the skin in the problem zones. The massage increases the blood supply, which improves the elimination of metabolic wastes. In order to break up the fat deposits, the technique involves pressing firmly and

kneading the problem zone area. Therefore, this kind of massage can be quite painful. If you have cellulite areas that are extremely pressure-

Wrapping, then sweating: Aromatherapy oil, heat, and compression wrapping cause fat reduction in the tissue.

sensitive, you should not have this kind of massage. The same holds true in the areas where you have varicose veins. It is important that the esthetician you go to is properly trained. You can get bruises if the wrong spots are pressed during the massage. The length and price of a session varies according to the spa and location. A 20-minute session can cost approximately $55–$100. You should see visible results after ten sessions.

Spa treatment #3: Suction-pumping massage

The principle is the same as cupping. Flasks of different sizes are placed one after another on the skin. Each of them is connected to a pump that draws the air out of the glass so that the skin is suctioned in. When the esthetician strokes the cellulite spots with the glass, blood supply increases, causing a strong warm feeling and a temporary red-

Pressotherapy: The tissue is unclogged in these inflatable boots through gentle pumping.

dening. This stimulates lymph flow and metabolism. When the treatment is done repeatedly, the walls of the fat cells are said to become so porous that fat is reduced. The suction-pumping massage must not be done on the areas where you can develop varicose veins, or if they are already there.

In order to achieve a visible result, you need about ten 30-minute treatments. The cost of a session varies according to the spa and location. It can be about $55–$75.

Spa treatment #4: Deep heat therapy

In this treatment, the problem zones are wrapped with heatable elastic bandages. Infrared rays warm up 1.2 inches (3 cm) deep into the tissue. The temperature reaches 104°F (40°C), and the body reacts by heating up an additional 2°. The heat accelerates the metabolism in the warmed skin regions so that fat is reduced there. The sweating flushes excess water out of the tissue. When this is repeated a sufficient number of times, supplemented by proper diet and

Laser light: Stimulates the collagen formation in the tissue.

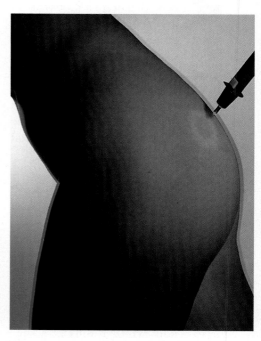

sports activities, this can lead to measurable results. The results, however, will only stay if you keep up these respective disciplines.

Doctors are rather skeptical about deep heat therapy. From a medical standpoint, you should avoid doing this on large surface areas if you have circulation problems, metabolism problems, weak

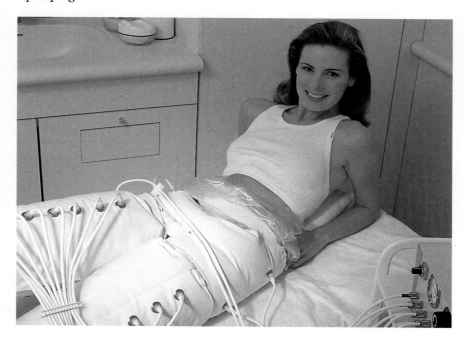

veins, kidney ailments, or thyroid ailments. In addition, there is the danger that this treatment can increase, instead of reduce, water retention and swellings in areas with a lot of cellulite.

You need at least ten 1-hour sessions to see any results. The cost varies according to the spa and location. A session can be about $30–$40.

Spa treatment #5:
Color-light therapy

Depending on the color, light waves penetrate differently into the skin to cause specific reactions. This principle is used in color-light therapy. Since violet light goes especially deep into the skin, underneath and into the fat tissue, it is used for the treatment of cellulite. It is supposed to stimulate metabolism and lymph flow, and unclog the tissue. This all assists a comprehensive anti-cellulite program that includes sports activity, proper diet, and massage.

You need at least twenty treatments in intervals of 2–3 days. A session usually lasts between 10 and 20 minutes. Costs vary according to the spa and location, and can be about $20–$25.

Spa treatment #6:
Laser treatment

A "soft" laser is used in this treatment. Its radiation is not as strong and concentrated as the kind used in surgery. A beam is emitted from a laser tool onto the cellulite area. It is supposed to stimulate the energy process and the collagen formation of the cells so that the tissue becomes tight again. This treatment, however, is not as effective on areas where there is a high concentration of cellulite. You probably need at least fifteen 45-minute treatments to see any visible results. The cost varies according to the spa and location. It can be about $500–$1000.

Spa treatment #7:
Herbal wraps

The problem zone areas are first massaged with herbal extracts or essential oils. Then they are wrapped with linen wraps or tight elastic bandages that have been soaked with or steamed in aromatic herbal blends. While those take affect for about 30 minutes, you need to sweat a lot either in the sauna or under infrared lamps.

The heat and the pressure of the wraps stimulate metabolism, which helps to reduce the fat in the tissue. Try to get this treatment every day for about 90 minutes a week. This therapy is not recommended if you have circulation problems and/or weak veins, such as spider veins or varicose veins.

Spa treatment #8:
Pressotherapy

This method of lymph drainage is done with electrically-produced air pressure waves. The problem zones are wrapped with cuffs (or the entire legs are put into inflatable boots). These cuffs contain inflatable air-chambers that are rhythmically filled and emptied out with air pressure. The pressure of the waves activates the lymph flow and unclogs the tissue, like the manual lymphatic drainage method. However, the results are usually less visible and do not last as long. One to two treatments per week, overall about fifteen, are recommended. The cost varies with the spa and location. It can be between $25 and $50.

WHICH TREATMENT REALLY WORKS?

There is no guarantee how successful each of the individual treatments are, since there is no scientifically founded research on them. Spas, however, report good results. In general, the results depend on the condition of the tissue being treated, the ability of the esthetician, and how disciplined the client is in supplementing the treatment with proper diet and exercise. Therefore, the chances and degree of success vary from client to client.

ELECTRIC STIMULATION

Electric stimulation therapy is a comfortable do-it-yourself method for activating the cellulite tissue.

For a long time, electric stimulation therapy was only used by professionals, for example in beauty spas. But, in the meantime, there are also devices that can be used at home. They are different from the professional ones only in that they have fewer connecting electrodes. That means while beauty spas can treat several parts of the body simultaneously, you can only treat the different parts of your body one at a time at home. Try to find a home device that contains as many electrodes as possible in order to be able to treat a greater surface area and achieve faster results.

All of the electric stimulation therapy devices, whether in spas or for private use, are meant to passively move the muscles at the problem zones (stomach, buttocks, upper thighs, and upper arms). The theory behind this device is that it induces strong muscular contractions in order to burn up energy supplied by the surrounding fat cells. As a result, the space for the fat cells also becomes more and more scarce where the muscles are tight.

How is it done?

Two or more electrodes are fixed with elastic bands to the body part that is to be treated. The plates have to be attached to the right and left sides of the body so that you will get symmetrical results. Electric cables, which are connected to the machine, are inserted into the plates. When the machine is turned on, current is then led directly to the muscle. It stimulates the muscle to contract and expand rhythmically. Depending on the frequency chosen, it can be up to two thousand times per minute. Intensity, speed, and duration of the impulses can be regulated individually for each plate.

Important: You should feel only a slight vibration. If it hurts, the current is too high.

The electric current is so weak that, if it is adjusted correctly, it should not damage the tissue. As a matter of fact, the gentle vibration has a relaxing effect. Therefore, it is best to use the electrodes in the evening before going to sleep. While the muscles "do their gymnastics," you can read, watch TV, or perhaps take a few steps (make sure though that the electrodes and bandages do not slide off).

A treatment should last at least three quarters of an hour. Only after about 2 weeks will you see the first visible results. But if you take a break from the treatment for a long period of time, the condition of the skin will revert to its old state again.

What else you should know?

■ Do not use electric stimulation therapy if you have varicose veins, inflammation and/or swellings, open wounds, or skin injuries (such as a sunburn). Also, do not use this treatment if you are pregnant. If you have a metal device in your body, e.g., a pacemaker, you should ask the doctor before using this treatment.

■ This treatment is less effective on very loose connective tissues. The effect is also less noticeable on athletic muscles.

■ The cost of a home electric stimulation device varies according to the model and the number of electrodes the model has. The more electrode connections it has, the more expensive the device is. It costs around $1200–$1500.

Passive isometric gymnastics: Electric stimulation, via electropads, is sent into the cellulite tissue.

Here is a suggested daily planner that incorporates all the various methods— anti-cellulite products, massages, hydrotherapy, and spa treatments—at optimal use. If you do not have the time to follow this strict schedule, you can make up your own plan that realistically fits your schedule and suits your own needs. But do not forget to look also at the training program on pages 86 and 87.

DAILY PLANNER

	Hydrotherapy
Monday	Morning: Warm and cool shower
	Evening: Sauna
Tuesday	Morning: Warm and cool shower
	Evening: Anti-cellulite bath
Wednesday	Morning: Warm and cool shower
Thursday	Morning: Warm and cool shower
	Evening: Sauna
Friday	
	Morning: Warm and cool shower
Saturday/ Sunday	Morning: Warm and cool shower

Massage	Anti-cellulite product	Spa treatment
Morning: Brush massage Evening: Passive muscle gym or massage	Morning: Anti-cellulite gel Evening: Rubbing with ice and anti-cellulite gel	Manual lymphatic drainage or another treatment
Morning: Tugging or rolling massage Evening: Passive muscle gym or massage	Morning: Anti-cellulite gel Evening: Anti-cellulite gel	
Morning: Brush massage	Morning: Anti-cellulite gel Evening: Herbal wrap, wheat grass pack, or another natural product treatment	
Morning: Tugging or rolling massage Evening: Passive muscle gym or massage	Morning: Anti-cellulite gel Evening: Rubbing with ice and anti-cellulite gel	*Sea salt baths are relaxing and help remove tissue sludge.*
Morning: Brush massage Evening: Passive muscle gym or massage	Morning: Anti-cellulite gel Evening: Anti-cellulite gel	Manual lymphatic drainage or another treatment
Morning: Tugging or rolling massage	Morning: Anti-cellulite gel Evening: Anti-cellulite gel	

CHAPTER II

TIGHTENING TI

Loose skin is also caused by flabby muscles. Therefore, muscle training is a must in order to tighten up the hips, buttocks, and upper thighs. Read which exercises and training equipment are the best when you're working out either at a gym or home. You may also want to follow an exercise program such as on pages 86 and 87.

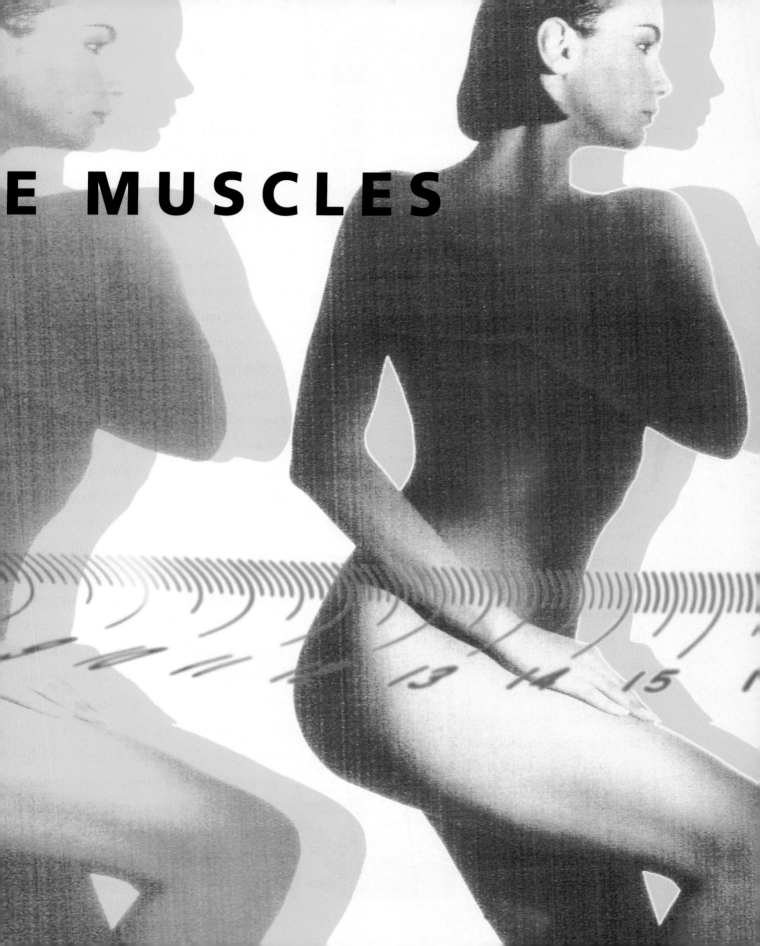

E MUSCLES

EXERCISING AT HOME

A cellulite workout program and using training equipment are two ways to tighten muscles.

It doesn't matter whether you prefer to exercise alone at home or with other people in a gym to get into the best physical shape. Either will give you the same results. Your decision to work out at home or in a gym should be determined by how often you will do it. Exercising regularly is the only way to achieve success.

What are the benefits of exercising at home?

Exercising in your own home is more comfortable. You can do it at your own convenience, you do not have to travel to the place where you'll exercise, and you do not have to pay a membership fee to use the gym. Yet, working out alone requires a great deal of self-motivation. You need to be disciplined to lie down each day at home on an exercise mat or work regularly on training equipment. In addition to that, you won't have an experienced trainer available to correct you on any mistakes you make, which can become habits and, as a result, possibly cause you injury.

In any case, exercising out must be done in conjunction with anti-cellulite products and proper nutrition. Any exercising is by all means better than doing nothing at all.

What are the different ways to exercise?

We offer three possibilities: First is what we called a "turbo gym" workout program, which aims specifically at the problem zones. It lasts for 4 weeks and contains only two exercises whose degree of difficulty increases from week to week (see pages 52–59). The second possibility involves working out with weights on your ankles. The movements of the legs, made more difficult with weights, aim also at strengthening the muscles of the stomach, buttocks, and upper thighs. Since more resistance has to be overcome because of the weights, the exercises done are especially exhausting, but also especially effective (see pages 60–61).

Some people are more motivated by purchasing training equipment (from simple gadgets to pricier machines), which specifically trains the muscular system of the problem zones (see page 62ff).

How can muscle training get rid of cellulite?

Targeting your exercise to certain areas decreases the amount of fat in those places because you are dramatically burning up energy there. The muscles build up and take up more space at the cost of the fat cells. As a result, the tightened tissue not only feels tighter, but it also looks tighter.

In addition, a trained muscular system is better supplied with blood, which promotes a faster removal of metabolic waste products. Removal of tissue sludge through muscle training also tightens the connective tissue and smooths the skin surface.

What should you keep in mind when exercising?

■ Sporadic but intensive exercising doesn't work, because the muscles need a regular workout to strengthen. Therefore, exercise for a short time, but often, rather than for a long time and infrequently. In order to see success, you must work out every day.

■ Don't work out until you're sore. Pain arises from tears in the fine branches of the muscle fibers.

As a result, the muscle swells and becomes hard. It tenses up and hinders circulation in the cellulite tissue.

■ Do not forget to warm up and cool down when you exercise alone at home. Ten or twenty jumps with a jump rope is a suitable warm-up. The rabbit exercise from yoga is a suitable cool-down: Kneel on the floor, bend your upper body forward, place your arms laterally backward, and breathe deeply. This is a position that allows you to relax for as long as it takes.

Why do muscles get flabby?

You could say that the muscular system is by nature "lazy." In any daily movement, only the necessary muscle fibers needed to perform the work are summoned by the nervous system. The remaining ones only come work when the ones, which have already been active, become tired. But this is seldom the case in everyday life. A large number of the muscles remain unused and, as a result, underdeveloped.

Exercise 1: For the stomach, legs, and posterior

Lie down on your back, angle your legs, and lock your hands behind the nape of your neck. Slowly lift your upper body by tensing up your abdominal and posterior muscles. While doing this, keep your neck and shoulders as loose as possible. Slowly count to ten and then lower the upper body. Do this twenty times.

Exercise 2: For the waist and hips

Lie on your side. Stretch out your lower arm and rest your head on it. Support yourself with the other hand in front of you on the floor so that your body remains steady. Bend both legs. Lift your upper leg slowly about 8 inches and then lower it. Do this twenty times. Then change sides and repeat this exercise.

TURBO GYM

A turbo workout program for the problem zones: Two exercises each day for 4 weeks. upper thighs, buttocks, and stomach will become tighter and your cellulite condition will improve.

■ <u>It does not matter whether you exercise in the morning or evening</u>. It would be good to do it in the morning *and* evening. If you also do a sport or bodybuilding, it would be even better.

■ <u>You do only two exercises every day</u>, but you do each at least twenty times. This should take 10–15 minutes.

■ <u>This turbo program lasts</u> 4 weeks and can then be continued by cutting the exercise time in half.

■ The basic structure of the exercises is the same, but the degree of difficulty increases each week.

■ <u>After 2–3 weeks, you will begin to see results</u>: All muscles in the

WEEK *1.*

TURBO GYM

The two workout exercises for the second week of training resemble those of the first week, but they are more strenuous because you must do them forty times, not twenty times.

■ Important: Think about what you're doing while you do these exercises slowly and carefully. Do not rush or do them haphazardly. Otherwise, you may do them wrong and risk injuring yourself repeatedly. And thinking about what you're doing will make you more in touch with your body and make exercising less boring.

■ <u>Exercise to music</u>, because people tend to exercise better while listening to it. It does not matter what kind of music. If you enjoy it, you will naturally follow its rhythm.

■ <u>Breathing correctly</u> supplies your muscles with enough oxygen. When you tighten your muscles, exhale through your mouth. When you relax, inhale through your nose.

Exercise 1: For the stomach, legs, and posterior
Lie on your back and fold your hands behind your neck. Bend your legs. Place your right calf on or slightly above your left knee. Tighten your abdominal and posterior muscles as you slowly lift yourself up with the help of these muscles. Turn your upper body slightly towards your right knee. Slowly count to ten. Then carefully lower your upper body and leg. Do this twenty-five times for each side.

Exercise 2: For the waist and hips

*Lie on your side. Stretch out your lower arm and rest your head on it. Support
yourself with the other hand in front of you on the floor so that your body
remains steady. Bend both legs. Lift your upper leg slowly about 16 inches and
then lower it. Do this forty times. Then change sides and repeat this exercise.*

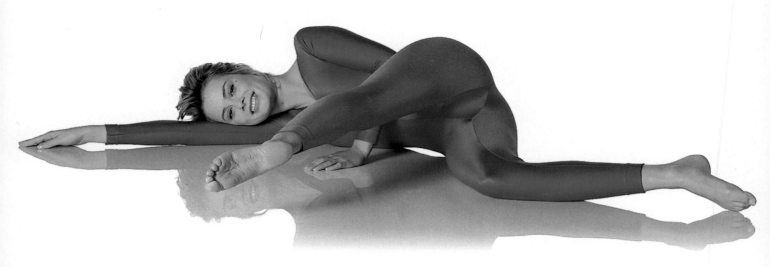

Exercise 2: For the waist and hips

Lie on your side. Stretch out your lower arm and rest your head on it. Support yourself with the other hand in front of you on the floor so that your body remains steady. Bend both legs. Stretch out your upper leg in front of you. In this stretched position, lift and lower your leg. Do this twenty times and then change sides.

Exercise 1: For the stomach, legs, and posterior

Lie on your back, bend your legs, and fold your hands behind your neck. Lift your upper body by tightening your abdominal and posterior muscles. Then turn your upper body slightly toward your right knee. At the same time, stretch your right leg upward with a straight knee. Bend your leg when you bring it down. Do this twenty-five times for each side.

TURBO GYM

The strength and condition of your muscles should have developed enough now for you to do these two exercises by the third week.

■ In principle, these are the same two <u>basic exercises</u> as before but they are <u>more intensified</u> and <u>more strenuous</u>.

■ As before, do these exercises <u>at least once but, if possible, twice a day</u>. The more you sweat, the better. It will help increase circulation and metabolism, which will decrease the amount of fat.

■ Since the exercises in the third week require considerably more muscle work and stretching, you should do <u>a brief warm-up before each exercise</u>. It is enough just to jump in place for 2 minutes or to use a jump rope to prepare your body for the strain.

WEEK 3.

TURBO GYM

Now the final part of the turbo program begins.

■ These last two exercises are <u>a bit acrobatic and rather strenuous</u>, but they really build up your muscles. By the way, the muscles that were worked during the 3 weeks are now getting their last finishing, which helps your posture.

■ As the degree of difficulty increases, it is <u>especially important</u> that the movements produce tension only in the area being worked on, and not the rest of your body.

For both of these exercises, press your shoulders down, make your neck long, and keep your back as straight as possible. And don't forget to breathe!

■ <u>Important</u>: When the fourth week is over, don't stop. Start from the beginning. In order to maintain what you have achieved, it is enough to do the exercises half as often the second time as the first.

WEEK 4.

Exercise 2: For the waist and hips

Lie on your right side. Stretch out your right arm and rest your head on it. Rest your left arm on your hip. Bend your legs. Now stretch your left leg and arm simultaneously upward and then lower them. Do this thirty times and then change sides.

Exercise 1: For the stomach, legs, and posterior

Like before, fold your hands behind your neck and bend your legs. But now, lift your hips off the ground by tensing up your abdominal and posterior muscles, and stretch one leg vertically upward with a straight knee. Move your hips up and down in this position twenty times while keeping the tension. Do not lower your hips all the way to the floor as you go up and down. Change legs.

WEIGHTS

Ankle weights offer advanced training and provide a change in your problem zone workout routine.

Working out on specific targeted areas is eight times more intensive when you incorporate weights/dumbbells. The additional weight makes the work harder for the muscles. They must use more energy and that also means burning up more fat.

consist of two plate-shaped weights that are tied with elastic bands to the left and right sides of your ankle.
■ Filled weights, which are more commonly sold in stores, are made of a soft, elastic material consisting of iron ore or some other

change the weight. Filled with water, it weighs about 5½ pounds (2½ kilograms). Filled with sand, it weighs about 7.7 pounds (3½ kilograms). With water plus sand, it weighs about 11 pounds (5 kilograms).

In the beginning, each weight should not be heavier than 1½ pounds (600 grams). Later on, you can increase it to 4–6½ pounds (2–3 kilograms) per weight. If you begin with too much weight, you will risk straining or pulling your muscles and overstretching your joints. In training your upper thighs, stomach, and buttocks, you need ankle weights. In general, there are three different kinds:
■ Plates (as shown in the photos on these two pages)

type of filling material. A Velcro fastener helps you secure them on. Others simply slip over your foot as a closed ring. Since they are very unobtrusive, you can wear them during aerobics or while you are jogging.
■ Hollow weights made of sturdy plastic are available in round and oval shapes. They have a split in the middle for you to put your foot through. The advantage of this type of ankle weight is that you can

For the posterior and upper thigh (above left):
Lie on your stomach. Alternate lifting and lowering your outstretched legs twenty times per leg.

For the front side of the upper thigh (above right):
Use your arms to support yourself in a sitting position. Alternate stretching out and bending back your legs thirty times per leg.

For the entire leg (left):
Position your body so that you are resting on your shoulders. Place your arms on the floor to help you maintain balance. Now extend and bend back your legs as if you are riding a bicycle. Do this twenty times per leg.

For the stomach (above):
Lie down on your back with your arms stretched out to the side. Lift your legs up into a V shape and then lower. Do this thirty times. As you do this, make sure that your back and the hollow of your back stay on the floor.

Training on a step stool: Ideal for tightening your posterior muscles and upper thighs.

Jumping rope: Still the simplest and most effective way to work your legs and get them into top shape.

Training with equipment at home: An alternative for anyone who doesn't want to do only floor exercises.

Sporting goods stores offer numerous fitness equipment, which you can use especially for the purpose of tightening your problem zones in your own home. Many of these fitness equipments are smaller and simpler than the ones used in gyms and fitness centers. If you use them correctly, you can get just as hard a workout and work up a good sweat. Detailed instructions and exercise suggestions usually come with the equipment. Some of them also have a videotape cassette with training programs available. To see any visible results, you should exercise 20 minutes each day. Any stepping, jumping, or gliding you do will be more fun if you do it to fast, rhythmic music.

With a ski machine, you make the same movements as if you're going down a ski slope. This tightens the hips, buttocks, and upper thighs.

Equipment #1: Step

Home and aerobic steps are miniature step stools, which are used in fitness centers for the "step class." The platform of the home version may be a little shorter than the ones used in the studios, but otherwise, there are no differences. Step training is especially good for the posterior and leg muscles. You are going up and down from the little stool (to the rhythm of good music) in quick, changing steps. The workout program is easy because there are only eight basic steps. The price varies according to manufacturer and where you buy it. It can cost around $100.

Equipment #2: Jump rope

Jumping rope tightens the entire muscular system of the legs. It is also excellent cardiovascular training and a stress reducer. You can use a simple jump rope made of nylon or hemp. There are fancier kinds made of plastic with a built-in counter for every rotation you do. It is important, though, that the rope be heavy enough to swing correctly and that it is the right length. In order to adjust the length, stand on the middle of the rope, straighten the rope, and fasten the handgrips to about the height of your chest. For jumping, it is best to wear ankle-high sneakers so that the ankle joints have good support. You can buy jump ropes for $15 or more.

Equipment #3: Ski machine

With a ski machine, you can make movements similar to the swaying motions done in skiing. You should wear sneakers that have good traction. The platform you stand on doesn't slide off because it rests on ball bearings that glide back and forth between two rubber strips. To balance yourself, hold a long pole, like a ski pole, in each hand. The

swaying movement mainly works the muscular system of the upper thighs. To work your abdominal muscles, you can sit down on the platform and sway from the center of your body. The price of ski machines varies according to model, manufac-

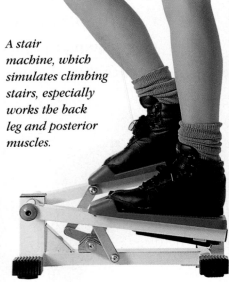

A stair machine, which simulates climbing stairs, especially works the back leg and posterior muscles.

turer, and where you buy it. It can cost around $200.

Equipment #4: Stair machine

Stair machines allow you to simulate the movements of climbing stairs. You stand on two plastic pedals and, without lifting your feet, alternate them up and down. The stair-climbing movement especially shapes up the buttocks and upper thighs. It is also a good cardiovascular exercise. To simultaneously work the muscular systems of the chest, back, and arms, you can select a stair machine in which ropes are attached for your hands to pull. You pull up against the resistance of each step. An additional advantage to this stair machine variation is air chambers in the treadmill. They

long. You wear "booties" with a slippery underside over your sneakers to help you glide back and forth on the board like a speed skater. You push off of the bumpers, which also prevent you from sliding off the board. Sliding intensively especially works the legs and posterior muscles. The price of a slide board varies accord-

The elastic bands of the "spider" can also be used work out the muscles of the upper thighs, stomach, and buttocks.

Gliding on a slide board strengthens and shapes the muscles up to your waist.

cushion the swing and make sure that your joints are not overstrained, even if you are doing an intensive workout. The price of stair machines varies according to model, manufacturer, and where you buy it. The cost is around $90–$3000.

Equipment #5: Slide board

A slide board is made up of a sheet of flexible or rigid plastic that is 6–8 feet

ing to model, manufacturer, and where you buy it. It can cost around $50–$100.

Equipment #6: Spider

This is a combination of elastic ropes that vary in length and can be attached together in various ways. Exercise suggestions usually come with every spider, including rope combinations for effectively working the problem zones. The cost is around $20.

If you don't have the discipline to exercise regularly at home alone, there are many ways to exercise elsewhere.

It does require a lot of willpower to make yourself work out—doing floor exercises, using weights, or equipment training—at home every day or every second day. Signing up for a weekly aerobics class, or joining a gym or sports club, may help you keep it up and stick with it. Being in a group environment, among people who are just as motivated as you are about working out, can actually increase your desire and motivation. The change of scenery from the office or house to a gym or sports club, in which you could be dancing or playing tennis, can also be another encouragement.

Possibility #1: Training in a fitness center

People in a fitness center are interested in working out. That means everyone is motivated to get into their best physical shape and look good. As a result, the environment en-

EXERCISING ELSEWHERE

courages you do the same as well. You work out to the best of your ability with people around helping and encouraging you. In a fitness center, you will find bodybuilding equipment and different kinds of aerobic classes that usually incorporate the latest trends and programs. See pages 72–77 for more about bodybuilding.

A good fitness center should offer these types of classes:

■ Water exercises in the swimming pool are an up and coming fitness trend. Exercising in the water is especially ideal for tightening the problem zones (see pages 69–71).

■ Workout classes, in which you are exercising in a group to rhythmic music, are not only good for your problem zones, but they are a great way of relieving stress, building your stamina, and increasing strength. Aerobics and its variations have been, and still are, the most popular classes around. Other variations can include step classes, in which you are jumping on and off a little step stool. Other slower, but just as strenuous, classes include special classes for problem zone areas, callanetics, Tai Chi, and other Eastern types of body training (see pages 79–81).

In order to exercise regularly and as often as possible, you should get at least a 3-month membership. Fees vary according to the fitness center, but the majority of them have relaxation equipment like saunas, solariums, and whirlpools.

Possibility #2: Training in a sports club

Many sports clubs offer almost the same training opportunities as fitness centers, usually at a lower price. Included here are fitness and conditioning gyms and classes for aerobics, circuit training (which focuses on the heart and lungs as well as muscles), judo, karate, and aikido. In addition to that, there are the usual group sports like basketball, handball, volleyball, and hockey as well as tennis and table tennis.

You can find a sports club through recommendation or from the telephone book.

Possibility #3: Power sport

If you want to train on your own schedule, as opposed to when classes are offered at a fitness center or sports club, you should pick a sport that works your legs and, in order to keep doing it, is also something you enjoy doing. In-line skating, a very trendy sport that looks like ice skating on wheels, is a good choice. Power walking, which is walking very quickly, is great for your upper thighs and posterior muscles. Finally, if you don't like either working out in a gym or doing any sports, you may consider taking a dance class. Most dancing usually concentrates on the problem zone areas—the hips, stomach, and buttocks. See pages 82–85 about power sports.

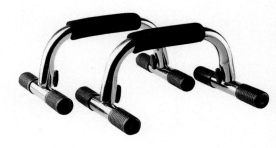

WATER EXERCISES

Water exercises are a great workout for the problem zones. They strengthen the muscles and massage the tissue.

Doing aqua aerobics or water exercises is less strenuous than working out on the floor but just as effective. Since the pressure of the water is fifty times stronger than that of the air, you must use more force for each movement you make. But the buoyancy in the water balances this out to such an extent that your overall moves are done with less effort. As a result, you are more relaxed and do not become out of breath as easily. And since you're in the water, you won't feel hot and sweaty, unlike working out in a gym. Also, the connective tissues get a wonderful massage from the pressure and movement of the water. That is very good, especially for cellulite.

How do you do water exercises?

Stand in the water up to your chest and, in general, do the same exercises as you would do on the exercise floor. Of course, you are moving slower because you

A new trend: Water exercising. Working with dumbbells, you exercise your arms, shoulders, chest, and the muscles of your problem zones.

have water resistance. Aqua step is especially effective for the problem zone areas. Little step stools are placed at the bottom of the pool floor and you do the same routine as in a regular step exercise class (see page 79).

Where can you exercise?

You can sign up for a water exercise program at a fitness center that has its own swimming pool, at a public pool facility that has a set time for training, or at swim clubs. The price for a water exercise program varies according to where you go. Whichever facility you choose, you should go at least twice a week to exercise. Swimming some lanes before and afterwards is a good way to warm up and relax.

Exercising at the pool's edge

A good alternative to the "in" sport of water exercising is simply working out on your own at the pool's shallow edge. Here, your legs and, thus, your problem zones' posterior muscles, upper thighs, hips, and stomach are exercised. Your hands and arms have enough work to do by just holding on. It's a good idea to swim first for 15 minutes, then do some exercises, then swim again.

A different step: Aqua step, an underwater but especially effective alternative to the step exercise on a gym floor.

Since you tend to shorten your movements in the water, pay attention when exercising that you make full and complete motions. It is also important that you tighten your abdominal muscles in order to keep your body upright. As in floor exercises, the success of your exercising rests on repetition. Do all your exercises at least twenty times. See the exercise suggestions on the right.

How do you protect your skin from chlorine?

Chlorine can irritate your skin and mucous membranes. Swimming goggles are a necessary part of your water training equipment. For skin protection, you can apply waterproof sun-milk after cleaning your body and before entering the pool. The sun-milk protects your skin from the sun (if it's an outdoor pool), and the emulsion protects and creates a screen between your skin and the water. There are also special shampoos and soaps for washing out the chlorine after you leave the pool. Shower with these products and then apply the sun-milk on your face and body.

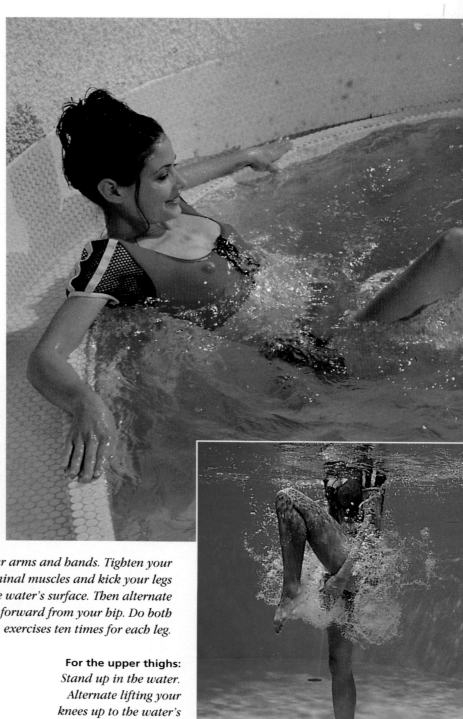

For the stomach:
Press your back against the edge of the pool and hold on with your arms and hands. Tighten your abdominal muscles and kick your legs close to the water's surface. Then alternate kicking forward from your hip. Do both exercises ten times for each leg.

For the upper thighs:
Stand up in the water. Alternate lifting your knees up to the water's surface and clapping your hands underneath the lifted leg. Do this ten times for each leg.

For the legs:

Walk through the water taking big steps. Each time, strongly swing forward the opposite arm against the resistance of the water. Do two sets of ten steps.

For the buttocks:

Stand facing the edge of the pool. Hold on to the edge with both your hands. Stretch one leg backwards, lifting it as high as possible and bouncing with small movements. Do this ten times per leg.

For the hips:

Stand beside the edge of the pool. Hold on to the edge or ladder with one hand and place your other hand on your hip. Stretch the outer leg far to the side and then make leg circles. Do this ten times and then change sides.

BODYBUILDING

The exercise equipment in fitness centers is excellent for targeting specific muscles.

A trainer, with whom you can discuss your goals (tightening your problem zones) at the beginning of your training, can decide how often you should work out at each machine. A trainer can also recommend how much weight to add on to each of the machines in order to make the exercise more difficult or more easy.

You should do your routine two to three times a week with at least a 48-hour break in between. Training every day is not a good idea, because it leaves the muscles that are worked too little time to recover.

There are abdominal machines for strengthening the abdominal muscles. But if your abdominal muscles need extra work, you should also do floor exercises. Many people exercising in fitness centers incorporate both a machine and floor workout in their routine.

ABDOMEN 1.

For the upper abdominal muscles:

Lie on your back with hands behind your head. Place your legs on a high enough box so that the lower legs are horizontal to the floor. Lift your upper body from your abdominal muscles. Look up to the ceiling. Do this fifteen times.

For the oblique abdominal muscles:

From the same starting position as in the first exercise, place one hand behind your head and stretch the other one to the opposite knee. This lifts the upper body diagonally. Do this fifteen times per side.

Working out at the abdominal machine:
Push the bar forward with your chest against the resistance of the weights. Bring your upper body slightly forward and then bring it back. When bending forward, you should feel a pull in your abdominal muscles. Do this twenty times with 20-pound (about 10-kilogram) weights.

For the lower abdominal muscles:
Lie on your back with your hands behind your head. Bring your legs up and cross them. Lift your upper

body from your abdominal muscles. Do this fifteen times. It is important that you point your chin to your knees.

For posterior and leg muscles:

Power walking on a treadmill is great for the legs and posterior. Especially exhausting is when you walk uphill. The degree of inclination can be adjusted as high as you like with the computer. Walk on the treadmill for at least 20 minutes. This is also a good warm-up.

For the muscles at the hip and outside of the posterior:

With an abductor machine, the weights are pressed upward when you spreads your legs wide apart. Important: Open your thighs slowly, evenly, and as wide as possible. Close them slowly as well. It is best to do three sets with twenty repetitions each time.

BODYBUILDING

For posterior, hip, and upper thigh muscles:
A stair machine simulates the climbing of stairs by treading on pedals. This also provides a good cardiovascular workout. You can program the machine to different programs and degrees of difficulty. The optimum training time is 15–20 minutes.

Most of the machines that work the posterior (buttock) and hip muscles also have a great effect on your legs. A good supplement to that are the two floor exercises mentioned below.

■ <u>Tip</u>: In the beginning, it is better to use less weights, but to do more repetitions. The best is to do three sets with twenty movements each, with only short breaks in between. If you want to intensify the training later on, increasing the repetitions is more effective than adding on more weights!

HIPS & POSTERIOR 2

For the posterior:
Get on the floor on your knees and elbows. Stretch one leg in an angle backwards and bounce upwards. Your back should remain as straight as possible. Do this twenty times per leg.

For the posterior:
Lie down on your back with legs bent and feet flat on the floor. Tuck in your buttocks up and down twenty times while tightening your abdominal and buttock muscles. Keep your neck loose!

BODYBUILDING

There are different exercise machines that target the front or back parts of the upper thighs. Exercising the upper thighs also works the muscular system of the hips and buttocks as well as the knees and lower legs. By the way, targeting specific muscles does not cause the fat to completely disappear from those areas. It does make the skin tighter and the cellulite less prominent.

■ Tip for training: Exhale each time as you tighten your muscles. Inhale deeply and slowly when you relax the muscles.

For the lower front upper thigh muscles:
Using a leg-curling machine, hold on to the sides and pull the bar upward with your lower legs. Then, without stopping, lower it slowly. It is best to do three sets twenty times each using 40-pound (about 20-kilogram) weights.

UPPER THIGHS 3

For the front upper thigh muscles:
Using a lying leg-press machine, push the weights forward with your legs while lying down so that your back remains straight. When you relax, draw your legs up to your body only until the tension subsides. Do this twenty times with 40-pound (about 20-kilogram) weights.

For the rear upper thigh muscles and posterior:
Using a leg-curling machine, rest your stomach flat on the bench and pull up the roller pad with your heels in the direction of your posterior. Do three sets twenty times each using 20-pound (about 10-kilogram) weights.

For the insides of the upper thighs: *Using an adductor machine, bring the pads together with your knees in a slow opening and closing rhythm. It is best to do three sets twenty times each using 40-pound (about 20-kilogram) weights.*

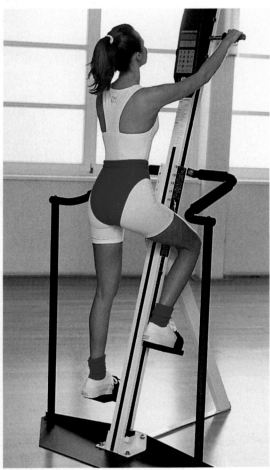

For upper thighs, posterior, and more: *A Versaclimber, an alternative to the stair machine (see page 75), works out and conditions 90% of your muscles. It has grips for your hands and feet to simulate the action and full-body motion of climbing. The optimum exercise time is 20 minutes.*

CLASSES

Most fitness centers and sports clubs offer classes that are specifically for tightening the problem zone areas.

"Abs, Buns, and Thighs" class

This special class works the muscular system of the upper thighs, stomach, and hip area. The exercises in these classes are done standing up or on floor mats. An Abs, Buns, and Thighs class can be strenuous, but also calming. With gentle music, you can make relatively slow movements. But in order for it to be effective, you need to repeat each exercise many times.

Another special class focuses only on the abs. Here, you only work the upper, lower, and oblique abdominal muscles.

Leg workout: Step class

A step class usually lasts an hour. Here, accompanied by dance music, you step up on and down from a small plastic platform. Therefore, a step class provides an excellent workout for the legs and posterior. The step is about 3 inches (8 centimeters) high, but its height can be adjusted according to the different types of exercises and the degree of difficulty. In order to work the upper body, you hold small

Your legs get a good workout whether you take a regular aerobics or specialized class.

HOW OFTEN DO YOU NEED TO EXERCISE?

To see any results, you must exercise two to three times a week.
■ **Where do you take classes?** At a fitness center, sports or athletic club, or through a university's continuing education department. Martial arts classes are taught in individual martial arts schools, sports clubs, and also through continuing education departments.
■ **What should you wear?** Sweats or a jogging outfit and sneakers with a good support. For aerobics, look for semi high-top sneakers that offer ankle support. Martial arts classes usually require special uniforms.

weights or dumbbells in each hand. A step class increases muscle buildup, flexibility, and condition. Since a step class is very tiring, people with no training should first build up their strength in another class.

Gentler workout: Callanetics

This program of exercises was developed by Callan Pinckney. The muscle training focuses on the area between the navel and knees so that the different muscle parts are worked out individually. The exercises consist of small concentrated sequences in which the respective parts of the body are moved back and forth no more than an inch (2 centimeters). But the exercises are repeated more often—up to a hundred times. People who do not exercise a lot can participate in callanetics, because the exercises are simple and easy on back and joints. And by exercising without music, everyone can go at their own speed.

Body workout and aerobics

Neither form of exercise is specifically meant to work on the problem zone areas but, nonetheless, both have an effect on the hips, stomach, posterior, and upper thighs when done regularly.
■ **Aerobics** incorporates stretching, jumping, and running exercises to energetic music. It takes care of your flexibility, endurance, and condition. It gives you a great cardiovascular work-

out. Beginners should probably start with a lower-impact form of aerobics.

■ <u>Variations of aerobics</u> are low- and high-impact workouts with different degrees of difficulty for beginning, intermediate, and advanced people. These programs usually include 10-minute running or walking stages.

■ A <u>body workout</u> is a mixed form of aerobics, stretching, and simple weight training. The exercises and muscle training are done with small dumbbell weights that weigh 2–6 pounds (1–3 kilograms). A body workout is, therefore, as effective as bodybuilding. At the same time, you build up your endurance and flexibility. Since longer running and jumping stages are usually omitted from a body workout, it is easier on the ligaments and joints than doing aerobics.

Intense leg work: Martial arts

Different kinds of martial arts, such as Aikido, Karate, and Tae Kwon Do, are superb ways of working out the problem zones. The intense leg work automatically effects the muscular system of the stomach and posterior. That not only tightens the entire contour of your body, but it also improves your posture and movement.

DIFFERENT MEMBERSHIP PLANS

Membership fees for different fitness centers can vary greatly. The prices depend on the location of the center, the kinds of equipment, the size of the center, and its image. In order to exercise regularly, you must sign up for a 3-, 6-, or 12-month membership. That way, you can take full advantage of all the things the center has to offer. If you don't plan to train much, you may be better off signing up for ten sessions. Before joining, it is important that you pay attention to the different terms of the membership. Some places have peak-hour membership and off-peak membership. Find out, for instance, whether you can pro-rate the length of your membership if you happen to be sick for a while or if you go away on a vacation.

Abs, Buns, and Thighs class in a fitness center: After an exhaustive leg-lift exercise, everyone stretches to relax the large muscle on the outside of the upper thigh.

*Doing martial
arts, like Tae Kwon Do,
enhances not only the leg muscles but
also your concentration and reaction time.*

*In an aerobics, body
workout, or callanetics
class, beginning warm-up
exercises are necessary for
loosening up muscles and
preventing injuries.*

Power walking and other sports that strengthen the legs are excellent ways of working the problem zones.

POWER SPORTS

It would be ideal if you could do an outdoor sports in conjunction with working out at home and training in the studio. Of course, you should choose a sport that works the muscular system of the upper thighs, hips, and buttocks. Fortunately, some of the newer fitness trends, such as power walking, offer an almost perfect workout for the problem zones.

You must exercise two to three times a week for at least half an hour each time. This way, the body uses up its fat deposits in the desired areas and changes them into muscle. In addition, you will automatically improve your strength and endurance as well as help relax and clear your mind. The air quality in which you exercise is also very important. The additional oxygen intake, which is necessary for burning fat in the body, should be free of pollutants, such as car exhaust fumes, etc.

Power sport #1: In-line skating

This sports trend, which has been around for a few years, is a blend of roller skating and ice skating. The in-line skates consist of polyurethane boots and four wheels

PUT ON YOUR HEART-RATE MONITOR!

In order for fat deposits to turn into muscles, your heart rate should not be too high or too low while you exercise. If possible, try always to keep it between 120 and 140 beats per minute. If your heart rate is too low, it means you're not using enough energy. If it is too high, the body burns the more readily available carbohydrates of your last meal instead of the fat in your body. The carbohydrates are used for the change of fat into muscle if there is proper energy consumption.

(for professionals, up to eight) that are mounted under the soles in a row. The movements are similar to those of ice skating and intensively work the leg and posterior muscles. Since the runner of an in-line skate is wider than the blade of an ice skate, in-line skating is easier to learn. You can also reach higher speeds. With practice, you can get up to 25 miles (40 kilometers) an hour.

■ What do you need for in-line skating? Besides the in-line skates (which can cost anywhere between $200 and $400, depending on the manufacturer and where you buy them), you also need protective gear in case you fall. This consists of knee and elbow pads, wrist guards, and a helmet to protect you from any abrasion, bruise, or joint injury. The knee and elbow pads as well as wrist guards cost about $20 a pair. A helmet can cost around $40.

Power sport #2: Race walking

This sport is also called power walking or speed walking. This method of walking fast works the muscular system of the posterior and upper thighs more than traditional jogging. Race walking is with some certainty the most effective, and cheapest, training specifically for the problem zones.

The walking technique is relatively simple: You walk in big, fast strides, but you always have one foot on the ground—as opposed to jogging. With each step, your foot rolls completely off the ground from heel to toe.

In-line skating, a popular fitness trend, is fun and tightens the problem zones.

You can recognize the technically perfect walker by the arm motion and posture: Bent elbows, arms swinging more strongly than when walking normally, and chin slightly lowered in the direction of the breastbone. To get the correct walking posture, it may help to imagine your navel shining forward like a headlight. That deepens and strengthens your stride. Walking stimulates circulation and the exchange of oxygen just as much as jogging, but it also has the advantage in that it is easy on the joints.

■ <u>What do you need for race walking?</u> You need a good pair of sneakers or walking shoes that have foot padding and support. There are special walking shoes that have a low, slanted heel, which cushions each step.

Power sport #3: Biking

By biking, we are specifically referring to mountain biking. Mountain bikes differ from regular bicycles by having thicker tires, reinforced frames, and up to twenty-one gears to make it possible to ride quickly through uneven, mountainous terrains. Biking through the mountain is more fun and less dangerous than riding through the traffic of a city.

Mountain biking: Good fitness training that tightens the problem zones.

Dancing: A strenuous leg workout that is good for the body and spirit.

Race or power walking: The simplest and best sport for beating cellulite and fat deposits at the problem zones.

Tennis: A classic sport for working the problem zones.

With the even bending and stretching of the legs, you can especially work the calves, upper thighs, and buttocks. In order to see fat change into muscle, you must bike often and regularly. The minimum you must do is twice a week for an hour.

■ <u>What do you need for biking?</u> Mountain bikes can cost from several hundred to $1000, depending on the quality of the bike and where you buy it. If you want to ride your mountain bike in the city, make sure that your bike has a light, fenders, and a carrier. If you ride a racing bike, you may want to get rid of extras to travel lighter. Wearing proper bicycling clothes will help you get a better ride out of your bike. Four-, six-, or eight-fabric panel cycling shorts (cost: $39–$85) give you less leg fatigue by offering good support. Other accessories include cycling shoes (about $100–$200) for good ventilation and grip on the pedal, padded gloves (about $20), and a helmet (around $40).

Power sport #4: Dancing

Even though you usually dance indoors, your legs can get a tremendous workout when you do fast, energizing dances. Doing salsa, mambo, or lambada three to four times in a row is at least as effective as 10 minutes of intense jogging. After some weeks, your legs will become noticeably stronger. Also, the muscular system of your hips, stomach, and buttocks will become visibly tighter, which is partly because of an improved posture. In addition to being in better physical condition, you will find yourself in a better mood and have more self-confidence. That is because hardly any other fitness training makes you sweat so much and, at the same time, is so sensuous and invigorating.

If you do not have a dance partner, or want to learn a dance that does not need one, you can try flamenco, belly dancing, or tap dancing. They are also good at working the problem zones. They especially exercise the muscles at the hip and pelvis area as well as the legs.

■ <u>What do you need for dancing?</u> For salsa, lambada, and mambo, all you need is an energetic dance partner. For flamenco, you need flamenco shoes or normal shoes with a firm heel. For tap dancing, you need shoes with metal taps at the soles (around $50+).

You learn to dance by practicing with a partner in a dancing school. Belly dancing, tap dancing, and flamenco are also taught in fitness centers or dancing schools. The price for dance lessons varies according to the different schools. Classes at night schools are usually less expensive.

Power sport #5: Tennis, squash, etc.

If you are not interested in the new sports and prefer a more classic one, you might try tennis or squash to work your legs and help your problem zones. Also, table tennis, played professionally, and group sports, like handball, volleyball, or hockey, in which you constantly exercise your legs, have a positive effect on your problem zones. But you need to do these sports regularly and for sufficient lengths of time. At the very least, you need to engage in your sport twice a week for half an hour to an hour. That way, body fat and sagging tissue will slowly change to firmer muscles.

■ <u>What do you need?</u> For tennis and squash, you should take private lessons in the beginning so that you do not learn wrong movements. You need tennis and squash shoes that have well-cushioned soles, and you need a tennis or squash racket. In the beginning, you do not need a top-of-the line tennis racket. It is important that the grip feels right and it is the correct weight. For group sports, you need to find a sports club that offers the sport you're interested in and wear proper attire for the activity.

TRAINING PLAN

Here is a suggested training plan that you can alter to your individual needs. It would be best to: do a daily turbo gym or weights workout in the morning, exercise at a fitness center or on home training equipment three times a week in the evening, and do a power sport three times a week in the evening. You will need to coordinate between your training plan and daily planner (see pages 46 and 47).

	At home
Monday	Morning: 10 minutes turbo gym or weights workout
Tuesday	Morning: 10 minutes turbo gym or weights workout
Wednesday	Morning: 10 minutes turbo gym or weights workout
Thursday	Morning: 10 minutes turbo gym or weights workout
Friday	Morning: 10 minutes turbo gym or weights workout
Saturday/ Sunday	

At the gym	Home training equipment	Power sport

Evening: 1½ hours bodybuilding + workout class or similar …

… or 20 minutes slide board, stair machine, step, or similar

Evening: ½ hour race walking, skating, dancing, or similar

Evening: ½ hour race walking, skating, dancing, or similar

Evening: 1½ hours bodybuilding + workout class or similar …

… or 20 minutes slide board, stair machine, or similar

Evening: ½ hour race walking, skating, dancing, or similar

Afternoon: 1½ hours bodybuilding + workout class or similar …

… or 20 minutes slide board, stair machine, step, or similar

Morning: ½ hour race walking or similar

LOSING

CHAPTER III

WEIGHT

Having excess water and fat
will not get rid of cellulite.
The active agents in certain
"power foods" will help you
lose weight. A short diet will
help speed the process. It
doesn't matter whether you
eat these power foods by
themselves or as part of a diet
plan (see pages 114–115).

LOSING WEIGHT WITH POWER

People with problem zones generally also need to lose some weight. What's best is a 10-day diet of power foods.

To get tighter contours around the posterior and hips, you need a nutrition plan that is meant to drain and tighten the connective tissues. As a result, you will also get rid of a few pounds. But keep in mind that there is no diet that affects only the hips, stomach, buttocks, and upper thighs. Unfortunately, it is usually the areas which you want to trim down that are the most resistant to dieting. That is because your body is used to a certain amount of fat and water deposits in the cells. But, nevertheless, there is no way to avoid a low-calorie nutritional diet program, as opposed to a diet in which you merely eat less. Even though you would become slimmer by eating less, it may not have the best effect on your body and connective tissues. The weight loss would also probably be temporary. By only eating less, you are not learning any new and better nutritional habits. As a result, you will most likely return to your old weight after the diet. Repeated crash diets will also increase your body's set point (see pages 10–11). Your body will learn to function with few calories and store everything, which is more than the set point, in its fat deposits as soon as you resume normal eating again.

A nutritional program, in which very specific foods are eaten, promises to be the best success in the case of treating problem zones. These foods must contain substances that:

■ tighten your connective tissue,

■ cleanse your body,

■ relieve hunger,

■ and raise your mood.

Six pounds less in 2 weeks

The diet that we have worked out for you guarantees both:

■ <u>Losing up to 6 pounds in less than 2 weeks</u> by consuming 1200 calories per day;

■ Recipes with power food that are rich in calcium, zinc, copper, selenium, and silicon. These substances are important, especially for the connective tissues, because they further its cleansing and tightening. In addition, all the power food recipes contain the essential nutrients in the best proportions. Plenty of fiber takes care of relieving and detoxifying the intestines and, thus, also the tissue.

Where is the power?

You will see what we mean by power food in the following pages. The diet plan, including the recipes, all contain power foods (see page 98ff).

First, try to follow these guidelines:

■ <u>Whenever possible, eat organically grown food for your anti-cellulite diet</u>.

The fewer damaging chemicals your food contains, the less toxins, which hamper the reduction of tissue sludge, get into your connective tissues.

■ <u>After your diet, try to keep eating these power foods</u>. Continue to use the recipes but increase the amount of the ingredients that are good for the connective tissue.

■ <u>Cut down on fat, sugar, alcohol, and meat</u>, because they further acid formation in the tissue. Eat more basic foods, such as fruits, vegetables, potatoes, milk and other dairy products, and fresh herbs.

■ <u>By following this nutritional guideline</u> you will be guaranteed the success of your diet and visible, lasting results at your problem zones.

POWER FOODS

Our cellulite diet is based on having the right active agents.

Where does the power in "power foods" lie? Not, as it usually does, in the calories, which provide strength. What we mean by power are the active agents that specifically reduce excess water and sludge in the tissue in the problem zones. The reduced calories of the diet at the same time cause the fat deposits in those areas to melt away. We have listed nine foods under the category of power food, because:

■ they are especially rich in cellulite-reducing substances;

■ almost everyone likes to eat them;

■ they can be bought everywhere, prepared without any problems, and are not expensive;

■ a diversified menu can be created with them—even after the diet;

■ some of them also contain a substance (serotonin) that can give you a little "high"—an effect that you need, especially during a diet.

POTATO

1. A potato is relatively high in potassium—a mineral substance that helps to eliminate excess water from the tissue.
2. It is also relatively high in copper. This helps the tightness and elasticity of the connective tissue.
3. It has a lot of fiber, which is vital for removing tissue sludge via the intestines.
Extra power points: It is high in vitamin C and has plenty of carbohydrates, which give you energy. It is also relatively high in protein, which is especially valuable when it is combined with animal protein (e.g., potato with egg). It is also low fat.
Shopping tips: Buy organically grown potatoes. They contain less chemicals and generally taste better. Potatoes that remain firm when cooked are best for salads and peeling; soft ones are best for mashed potatoes, soups, and potato flour.
Preparation tips: Cook the potatoes unpeeled, because the vitamins and minerals are directly under the skin. Remove the green spots, because they contain poisonous solanin.

Active agents in 3½ ounces of potato:

443 mg potassium
.15 mg copper
2.5 g fiber
22 mg vitamin C
18 g carbohydrates
2 g protein
.1 g fat

AVOCADO

1. The potassium in an avocado accelerates the elimination of excess water in the tissues.

2. The copper helps tighten loose connective tissue.

Extra power points: Avocado is high in magnesium, which activates more than three hundred enzymes, and unsaturated fatty acids, which are important for the proper metabolism of fat. In addition, avocados are high in vitamin D (essential for strong teeth and bones) and vitamin B6 (for carbohydrate and protein metabolism).

Shopping tips: When avocados are at their perfect degree of ripeness, you can press in the skin a little bit. Fruits with brown spots are overripe and not edible anymore. Hard, unripe avocados can, if necessary, be wrapped (in newspaper) and left to ripen on the radiator or in the sun.

Preparation tips: Cut avocados only shortly before you eat them, since the fruit pulp turns brownish in the air. Trickling lemon juice on the avocado stops discoloration and adds additional vitamins.

Active agents in 3½ ounces of avocado (about ½ fruit)

503 mg potassium
.21 mg copper
29 mg magnesium
.005 mg vitamin D
.5 mg vitamin B6
3.7 g carbohydrates
1.9 g protein
23.5 g fat

MILLET

Unprocessed millet is especially good for people with weak connective tissues:

1. It contains silicon, which helps build skin, teeth, and bones. It makes the connective tissue firmer and is good for hair and nails.

2. It is high in copper, which provides additional firmness and elasticity of the tissue.

3. It is very high in fiber, which gently cleans out the intestines.

Extra power points: It is very high in iron, which binds oxygen in the blood, and it can be very well utilized in combination with vitamin C. In addition to that, millet abundantly provides fluorine (for teeth), magnesium (for nerves), and manganese (for enzymes and hormones).

Shopping tips: When you buy millet products (grains, flour, flakes, noodles), pay good attention to the expiration date, since millet gets rancid quickly.

Preparation tips: Millet's slightly bitter taste disappears if you pour boiling water over the grains before preparing them, or if you dry roast them. Then cook 1 part millet with 1½ parts water for 10 minutes. Let it absorb more moisture briefly afterwards.

Active agents in 3½ ounces of millet:

40 mg silicon
.85 mg copper
3.8 g fiber
9 mg iron
170 mg magnesium
.04 mg fluorine
1.9 mg manganese
72.8 g carbohydrates
10.6 g protein
3.9 g fat

BROCCOLI

1. The potassium in broccoli works with sodium to control the body's water balance.
2. Its copper takes care of the elasticity and firmness of the connective tissue.
3. Its zinc fights and prevents the formation of free radicals. It is necessary for protein synthesis and collagen formation.
4. Its fiber cleans out the intestine and removes certain toxic metals from the body.
Extra power points: It is also high in vitamin C (strengthens the immune system), vitamin A (is good for the skin), folic acid (takes part in cell formation), calcium (builds up bones), magnesium (activates the different enzymes), iron (binds oxygen in the blood), manganese (detoxifies the body), iodine (is good for the thyroid), and glucosinolate (helps reduce the risk of some cancers).
Shopping tips: Buy the broccoli that have dark green little flowers. Avoid the yellow-green ones.
Preparation tips: Peel the bottom stems and cut the larger stems in half. Cook them in a little water for at most 10 minutes. They must not become mushy.

**Active agents
in 3½ ounces
of broccoli:**

*410 mg potassium
.94 mg zinc
.2 mg copper
3 g fiber
110 mg vitamin C
.32 mg vitamin A
113 mg calcium
24 mg magnesium
1.3 mg iron
5.8 g carbohydrates
3.5 g protein
.2 g fat*

BARLEY

1. Barley has a lot of silicon, which helps strengthen the connective tissue, hair, and nails.
2. It is high in zinc, which builds up connective tissue.
3. Its selenium protects against free radicals and, thus, helps prevent cancer.
4. Its water-soluble fiber forms gels and keeps your stomach full longer. It also stimulates the excretion of undesirable substances via the intestine and, thus, reduces the cancer risk for the large intestine.
Extra power points: It is high in iron (transports oxygen out of the lungs into the blood), magnesium (prevents muscle cramps and is important for the functioning of the nerves), and manganese (supports the immune system).
Shopping tips: Whole-grain barley is more nutritious than pearl barley, because the pearl barley has the bran removed.
Preparation tips: Soak the barley for 10 hours. Then cook it with 2½ times the amount of water for an hour. Let it absorb more moisture afterwards.

**Active agents
in 3½ ounces
of barley:**

*188 mg silicon
3.1 mg zinc
0.1 mg selenium
9.8 g fiber
2.8 mg iron
114 mg magnesium
1.7 mg manganese
73.1 g carbohydrates
10.6 g protein
2.1 g fat*

SAUERKRAUT

1. Sauerkraut is high in potassium, which eliminates excess water.

2. It has copper, which strengthens the tissue.

3. Its fiber helps to clean out the intestine.

Extra power points: Sauerkraut has a lot of vitamin C (protects against infectious diseases) and folic acid (cell formation). The lactic acid regenerates the colon bacteria and prevents fermentation. It also detoxifies and cleans out the digestive paths, which eliminates the formation of cancer-causing substances in the intestine.

Shopping tips: Lactic-acidically fermented sauerkraut is available in health-food stores and shops that sell natural products. Sauerkraut from a can is usually quite salty. Therefore, if possible, buy open sauerkraut.

Preparation tips: Do not wash sauerkraut or else you will lose too many active agents. Raw sauerkraut provides the most minerals. However, steaming sauerkraut loses about 23% of the vitamin C it has. Caraway seeds, marjoram, and cloves make the sauerkraut more palatable.

Active agents in 3½ ounces of sauerkraut:

288 mg potassium
.09 mg copper
2.2 g fiber
20 mg vitamin C
.02 mg folic acid
4.6 g carbohydrates
1.5 g protein
.3 g fat

MUSHROOMS

1. Mushrooms are high in potassium, which helps water balance.

2. They have copper, which supports the tissues.

3. They also have selenium to block free radicals.

Extra power points: Mushrooms are high in iron (for oxygen binding) and iodine (for the thyroid). They also have many vitamins, including vitamin D (for bone structure), niacin (for proper functioning of the stomach-intestinal tract), and pantothenic acid (for regulation of the metabolism of the skin cells).

Shopping tips: Buy only fresh mushrooms that have an intense smell, dry skin, and closed caps. Canned mushrooms contain less vitamins, and more lead and mercury.

Preparation tips: Do not wash mushrooms. Rub them off with a kitchen towel, because they will lose their aroma otherwise. They can be stored for a few days in an open bowl in the refrigerator. Cooked mushroom dishes that are cooled immediately can be heated up one more time.

Active agents in 3½ ounces of mushrooms:

418 mg potassium
.4 mg copper
.007 mg selenium
1.9 g fiber
1.1 mg iron
.018 mg iodine
.002 mg vitamin D
4.7 mg niacin
2 mg pantothenic acid
2.6 g carbohydrates
2.7 g protein
.3 g fat

BANANA

1. A banana has potassium to help eliminate excess water from the tissue.

2. It has plenty of silicon to help the formation of collagen for the connective tissue.

3. It has plenty of fiber to help clear out the intestines thoroughly.

Extra power points: A banana helps fill you up quickly and for a long time. It is high in the "happy chemical" serotonin, which satiates hunger and helps put you in a good mood. Tryptophan, an essential amino acid in bananas, also helps stabilize mood and is a natural sedative. In addition to that, bananas are high in magnesium (for enzymes and nerves), iron (for oxygen binding), manganese (for hormones), and vitamin B6 (for protein processing and the immune system).

Shopping tips: Yellow fruits contain 70% more vitamin C than green ones. Dark spots and mushy spots do not indicate a lack of quality. Do not put bananas in the refrigerator. Otherwise, they become black easily and cannot develop their aroma.

Active agents in 3½ ounces of bananas:

382 mg potassium
8 mg silicon
3 g fiber
36 mg magnesium
.7 mg iron
.53 mg manganese
.37 mg vitamin B6
24.4 g carbohydrates
1.1 g protein
.2 g fat

SPINACH

Spinach has, among other active anti-cellulite agents, a lot of potassium, which controls the body's water balance.

Extra power points: Spinach is a rather good supplier of calcium (for bone structure), magnesium (for nerves), iron (for oxygen), manganese (for enzymes), fluorine (for teeth), iodine (for thyroid), vitamin A (for eyes), folic acid (for cell formation), and vitamin C (for resistance to infection).

Shopping tips: Buy fresh spinach only in season so that the nitrate content is not too high. Frozen spinach often is of better quality, since it loses at the most 20% of its vitamin C content when frozen. When it is not stored well, it is often loses 50%.

Preparation tips: Since spinach contains a lot of oxalic acid, which inhibits calcium absorption, you should eat foods that contain more calcium (milk, cheese) the same day. Only lightly cook spinach. Otherwise, its nitrates will change into nitrites, which, in combination with amines, form carcinogenic nitrosamines.

Active agents in 3½ ounces of spinach:

633 mg potassium
126 mg calcium
58 mg magnesium
4.1 mg iron
1.76 mg manganese
.11 mg fluorine
.01 mg iodine
.82 mg vitamin A
.08 mg folic acid
51 mg vitamin C
2.4 g carbohydrates
2.5 g protein
.3 g fat

POWER KILLERS

Eating sweets can ruin the effects of even the best power foods and diet.

These are some of the power killers: Butter-cream and heavy-cream tarts; ice cream, chocolate mousse, custard, chocolate, lemonade, and soft drinks.

Everyone craves something sweet. Some people grow out of the craving. Others crave it more as they grow older. Sweets easily give you a lift or high. Serotonin, one of the neurotransmittors used by the brain, is formed from tryptophan and functions as a mood uplifter. Tryptophan, however, relies on insulin, which is emitted from the pancreas when we eat carbohydrates, e.g., sweets, bread, pasta, potatoes, etc. In principle, there should be nothing wrong with this because being in a good mood is healthful. But what matters is the type of carbohydrate that is being metabolized. If it is denatured sugar that does not have any vitamins and fiber, the body has a source of immediate energy that can be exhausted in 10 minutes at most. The blood sugar level then dips and the body again craves more sweets, thus beginning a vicious cycle. Luckily, not only "empty" carbohydrates like cakes, chocolate, and doughnuts achieve this euphoric effect, but complex carbohydrates in such items as whole-grain products do, too. You can tap into this serotonin source in your diet as well. Even though it takes a little bit longer for the blood sugar level to increase, it does not decrease as quickly. You can remain full and satisfied longer. Our anti-cellulite diet contains everything that is needed to keep the blood sugar up. In order to maintain this after your diet,

■ eat as many whole grain products and other power foods as possible,

■ have several small meals a day so that the blood sugar level does not go down too much,

■ have fresh fruit or dried fruit that is untreated with sulfur on hand in case you should have a craving for something sweet (see in-between meals on page 110),

■ regularly incorporate a small amount of some "unhealthy" sweet into your daily eating plan in order to slowly wean yourself off it.

A SWEETENING AGENT IS NO SUBSTITUTE

Even though sweetening agents save calories, they stimulate appetite. When you regularly eat products that are sweetened with sweetening agents, your body realizes that it is being tricked and does not supply any insulin. But that also means that no serotonin can be produced. Your mood will sink. Other sugar substitute substances like sorbitol or xylite are not alternatives, since they also have as many calories as sugar.

All the recipes in this anti-cellulite diet contain at least one power food.

DIET RULES

Diet rule #1: Eat alternately cold and warm

Choose from the list of recipes on the following pages one cold and one warm meal each per day, one breakfast, and two in-between meals. The cold recipes have 300 calories, the warm ones have 400, the breakfasts have 300, the in-between meals have 100 calories each. That means you will have 1200 calories a day. This will allow you to slowly and safely lose 4–6 pounds (2–3 kilograms), depending on your body condition, without depriving yourself of the essentials nutrients.

Diet rule #2: Eat as you wish or from a plan

Which warm or cold meal you choose each time is up to you. That means, it does not matter whether you have the millet meal as your warm meal for 2 days in a row or the avocado snack as a cold meal three times in a row. Yet each power food should be eaten at least twice during the diet.

■ If you prefer to follow a plan, you can follow a suggestion for the best sequence of meals from a complete diet on pages 114–117. There is also a shopping list that accompanies it (see pages 118–119).

Diet rule #3: Stick with it for 10 days

Eat the meals prepared according to the recipes from the anti-cellulite diet for at least 10 days. If possible, stay with these power foods after the diet so that you can maintain your success and keep the visible results. It should not be too difficult to eat as an in-between meal such power foods as a banana, avocado, or, once in a while, a peeled potato (see page 92). Millet, broccoli, spinach, and mushrooms can be creatively added to your usual menu as well.

■ All recipes are calculated for one person and can be increased after the diet without any problems (see pages 100 and 104). If you cook for your family as well, make about one and a half times the amount for one person.

■ If you work, have the warm meal in the evening and eat the cold meal for lunch. None of the recipes require great cooking skills or a lot of time. Generally, the warm meals can be prepared in 30 minutes. The cold snacks are ready even faster and can be easily prepared the night before.

Diet rule #4: Eat as many vegetables as you like

You should strictly adhere to the amounts given for the recipes so that the ratio of nutritional agents is correct. But in regards to vegetables, you can eat as much as you like—more than the recipes prescribe. Several more ounces will have no effect because those few extra calories will do nothing. The additional vitamins and minerals, however, are extremely useful because they can balance out any possible deficiency caused by a lack of quality or freshness. Of all foods, vegetables have the most nutritional agents.

That means the best ratio of active agents and energy content.

Diet rule #5: Measure instead of weighing

Seeing how much you weigh is not a good indication of the success of your diet, because your body weight does not depend only on how much you eat. Hormone variations, for example, cause in many women daily weight differences of up to 4 pounds. In addition, a scale does not distinguish between what is fat and muscle mass. If you work out a lot, you can build up muscles that weigh more than fat. However, your hips will look slimmer and tighter. It is better to use a measurement tape once a week for your waist, hips, and upper thighs. It is a more accurate indication of your success than a scale.

300-CALORIE SNACKS

These ten cold power-food snacks are great as lunches for work.

Here are some important tips for buying, preparing, and bringing food as snacks to work.

■ <u>Wash and clean fresh leaf salads and uncooked salad vegetables</u> the night before, but do not pour the dressing over them. Put the already mixed dressing into a little container and pour it over the salad the next day at noon shortly before you eat.

■ <u>If the salad has cooked ingredients,</u> mix it the night before with the dressing so that they will mix well.

■ <u>To avoid spilling,</u> carry your salads/snacks in plastic containers that are available in any houseware/department store. They are available in different sizes and qualities.

■ <u>Keep a plate at work</u> for you to put your food on. This will make your eating a more appetizing and pleasurable experience. Keep salt and pepper somewhere in your desk.

■ <u>If you like the snacks,</u> you can increase the recipes after the diet by half the portion. Even simpler: Keep the amount and eat a slice of whole grain bread with some cheese or butter on it.

Made fast, but not a fast food: A barley burger

RADISH AND POTATO SALAD
5¼ ounces potatoes, 4 tablespoons vegetable broth (ready made), 1 teaspoon oil, 1 tablespoon vinegar, ½ teaspoon mustard, salt, pepper, 1 hard-boiled egg, a bunch of radishes, as much cress as you like, 1 whole wheat cracker, 1 teaspoon butter

BARLEY BURGER
1 whole grain roll, lettuce leaves, 1 tomato, 1 barley patty (see Tip 1 below)

Cut the roll in half. Put in two washed and dried lettuce leaves. Add the barley patty and two slices of tomato.

■ Anti-cellulite active agents: Silicon, zinc, selenium, fiber

Tip 1: Have the "Barley patty with pepper salad" (see page 105) warm meal the night before. The ingredients for the recipe are enough to make three patties. You can eat two of them warm for dinner and leave the third for your barley burger.

Cook the potatoes, peel them, and then cut them into slices. Mix the vegetable broth with oil, vinegar, and spices. Pour it over the potatoes while they are still warm. Cut the hard-boiled egg into cubes and mix it, together with the radishes, which are cut into slices, with the cooled salad. Garnish with cress. Serve with a buttered whole wheat cracker.

Anti-cellulite active agents: Potassium, copper, fiber

Tip: This noon snack can be well prepared the night before (together with the warm "Unpeeled potatoes with tomato" meal) and eaten at work. Separately carry the salad, whole wheat cracker, and butter.

BROCCOLI SALAD

9 ounces broccoli, 2 teaspoons raisins, 1 tablespoon apple juice, fresh basil, garlic, salt, pepper, nutmeg, 1 teaspoon oil, 2 tablespoons vinegar, 4 tablespoons vegetable broth (ready made), 2 tablespoons pine nuts, 1 slice whole-grain bread

Clean the broccoli, cut it into small pieces, and cook it in a little water until it is firm but not too soft. Pour apple juice over the raisins and let them soak briefly. Chop up the basil and mix it with the spices, oil, vinegar, and vegetable broth to make a salad dressing. Pour it over the warm broccoli. Sprinkle the soaked raisins and pine nuts over it. Have it with whole-grain bread.

■ Anti-cellulite active agents: Potassium, zinc, copper, fiber

Tip 1: Instead of pine nuts, you can have roasted sunflower seeds.
Tip 2: If you have this salad for lunch at work, skip the garlic.
Tip 3: The water that the broccoli was cooked in contains valuable minerals. Use it as vegetable broth or drink it in the morning as a detoxifying drink!

STUFFED AVOCADO

½ avocado, 2 ounces mushrooms, 1 teaspoon oil, 1 tablespoon vinegar, garlic, salt, white pepper, 2 ounces watercress

Scoop out the inside of the avocado with a spoon. Cut the pulp into cubes and the mushrooms into slices. Combine the oil, vinegar, and spices into a salad dressing. Mix it with the avocado pulp and mushrooms and then pour them into the hollowed-out avocado. Garnish with watercress.

■ Anti-cellulite active agents: Potassium, copper, selenium, fiber

Tip 1: Leave the pulp in the other half of the avocado. Sprinkle some lemon juice over it so that it does not discolor. Cover it with foil and

Tip 2: Buy only real whole grain rolls. Many rolls contain only some crumbs of coarse grain and are merely dyed dark. If you can, find out the amount of whole grain. It should be at least 90%.

keep it in the refrigerator.

Tip 2: If you are unable to get fresh watercress, you can get it frozen. Both contain a lot of vitamin C, calcium, magnesium, iron, manganese, and hardly any calories.

BARLEY COOKIES WITH CUCUMBER

1 ounce barley grain, 3 ounces water, 3 tablespoons rolled oats, ½ egg, salt, pepper, curry, thyme, 1 teaspoon shortening, 3½ ounces cucumber, 3 tablespoons yogurt (1% fat), lemon juice, white pepper, dill

Soak the barley overnight in 3 ounces of water. Then boil it in that water for about an hour and let it absorb more moisture afterwards. Mix the barley with the oats, egg, and spices. Place two flat clusters with a tablespoon into a hot pan and fry them at medium heat, well covered. Turn them over after about 2 minutes. Cut the cucumber into slices. Season the yogurt with lemon juice, white pepper, and dill to make the sauce.

■ Anti-cellulite active agents: Silicon, zinc, selenium, fiber

Tip 1: Fry two or four times the amount of barley cookies to have them later on. Freeze them.

Tip 2: While you are getting ready in the morning, you can cook the barley. Then, in the evening, all you need to do is mix and fry it.

MILLET CREAM WITH FRUIT

4½ ounces skim milk (1% fat), cinnamon powder, .7 ounce millet flour, 1 teaspoon maple syrup or honey, 1 peach, 1 plum, 2 ounces grapes, 3 cherries (or another fruit of your choosing), lemon juice, 1 teaspoon chopped walnuts

SAUERKRAUT WITH GRAPES

3 ounces purple grapes, 5½ ounces fresh sauerkraut, 1 teaspoon cold-pressed sunflower oil, 2 tablespoons apple juice, 1 teaspoon lemon juice, 1 teaspoon honey, salt, white pepper, 1 teaspoon walnuts, 1 whole-grain roll

Cut the grapes in half and take out the seeds. Mix them with the sauerkraut, which is chopped into small pieces. Mix the oil, apple juice, lemon juice, honey, salt, and pepper. Then pour it over the salad. Sprinkle with chopped walnuts. Have it with a whole-grain roll.

■ Anti-cellulite active agents: Potassium, copper, fiber

Tip 1: Instead of sunflower oil, you can use safflower oil or another cold-

pressed oil with unsaturated fat.

Tip 2: If it is not the season for grapes, use a grated apple with a carrot or an orange. Also, pineapples and sour cherries taste good with sauerkraut.

AVOCADO WITH YOGURT SAUCE

½ avocado, lemon juice, 3½ ounces yogurt (1% fat), 1 teaspoon crème fraîche, lemon juice, plenty of parsley, salt, white pepper, 1 tomato

Peel the avocado, cut it into slices, serve it on a plate, and sprinkle some lemon juice over it so that it does not discolor. Mix the yogurt with the crème fraîche, lemon juice, finely chopped parsley, salt, and white pepper. Pour it over the avocado. Cut the tomato into cubes and add them to it.

■ Anti-cellulite agents: Potassium, copper

Tip 1: Parsley contains a lot of vitamin C and silicon. Since it has hardly any calories, you do not have to skimp on parsley.

eat the milk with cinnamon. Then
rinkle finely ground millet flour into
Cook for 2 minutes, let it absorb
ore moisture afterwards, and sweet-
it with maple syrup or honey. Cut
e fruit into small pieces, sprinkle
me lemon juice over them, and serve
a plate. Pour the millet cream over
em and sprinkle with walnuts.

Anti-cellulite active agents: Silicon,
pper, fiber

1: Use 9 ounces of fruit that is in
ason. Add in bananas if you want to
d more "power" to your meal.

2: Squeezing your own lemon juice
better than buying lemon juice from
tore. Keep it in a tightly sealed glass
ntainer will last for some days.

MUSHROOMS WITH FIELD LETTUCE

*1 kohlrabi, 3½ ounces mushroom,
1 teaspoon butter, 2 ounces field
lettuce or spinach, 1 teaspoon oil,
2 tablespoons balsamic vinegar, salt,
pepper, nutmeg, 2 tablespoons sunflower seeds, 1 whole wheat cracker*

Peel the kohlrabi, cut it into slices, and steam it for 3 minutes. Clean the mushrooms, cut them into small pieces, and fry them for a short time in butter. Wash and clean the field lettuce and serve it with the kohlrabi, which has cooled off, and mushrooms. Prepare a sauce by mixing the oil, vinegar, salt, pepper, and grated nutmeg. Pour it over the salad. Dry roast the sunflower seeds in a frying pan, let them cool off, and sprinkle them over the dish. Eat the whole wheat cracker with it.

■ Anti-cellulite active agents: Potassium, copper, selenium, fiber

Tip: It is easy to take this meal to work. Put the field lettuce with the kohlrabi and mushrooms in one container and the sauce in a separate container.

Tip 2: Take the avocado and the sauce with the tomato cubes separately wrapped to work.

SPINACH WITH CHICKEN BREAST

1 chicken breast fillet (about 3 ounces), 1 teaspoon oil, salt, pepper, 1 slice of bread, 1 teaspoon crème fraîche, 1 teaspoon vinegar, ½ teaspoon oil, ginger powder, pepper, 2 ounces small spinach leaves, 1 carrot

Brush the chicken breast fillet with oil and fry it for 5 minutes on each side in a coated frying pan. Flavor it with salt and pepper. Spread crème fraîche on the bread. Mix the vinegar and oil with ginger powder and pepper. Mix this with the washed raw spinach leaves and place it on the bread. Cut the chicken breast into slices and place it on the bread. Grate the carrot over it.

■ Anti-cellulite active agent: Potassium

Tip: Instead of a chicken breast fillet, one can use a small turkey cutlet or two slices of pork fillet or sliced beef (3 ounces each).

These ten warm power-food meals are ideal for dinner and ready in 30 minutes.

What you need:

■ <u>The necessary ingredients.</u> If you have any problems with this, follow the diet plan on pages 114–117 and use the shopping list that accompanies it.

■ <u>A frying pan that is coated or made of high-grade steel</u> so that you only have to brush it with a little olive oil, coconut oil, or butter.

■ <u>Use natural grains.</u> You can get them in health-food stores and natural-food stores.

■ When you buy vegetables and mushrooms, pay attention to <u>freshness</u> and buy, if possible, <u>organically grown products</u>. Try not to store them for a long time; otherwise, they will lose their freshness.

■ <u>If necessary, buy frozen products.</u> But make sure that no fat, modified starch, or flavor enhancers are added.

■ <u>Do not buy canned products!</u> They contain less vitamins and minerals, but more salt, which works against the active agent potassium.

■ <u>After the diet,</u> increase all the ingredients by half as you did for the cold snacks.

Making your power-food lunch the night before saves time.

400-CALORIE MEALS

STIR FRIED MILLET AND BROCCOLI
14 ounces millet, 4½ ounces vegetable broth (ready made), ½ rod of leek, 1 teaspoon shortening, 7 ounces broccoli, 1½ ounces vegetable broth (ready made), salt, cayenne pepper, grated nutmeg, 2 tablespoons crème fraîche, 1 tablespoon lemon juice

SWEET MILLET WITH RASPBERRRIES
14 ounces millet, 4½ ounces skim milk (1% fat), 1 egg, 1 tablespoon honey, salt, vanilla extract, lemon peel (untreated), 1 teaspoon shortening, 5 ounces fresh or frozen raspberries

Dry roast the millet in a small pot until it has a nice aroma. Pour milk over it. Let it simmer for 30 minutes at low heat and then let it absorb more moisture afterwards. Beat the egg yolk with the honey mixed in until it is creamy. Mix the cooked millet into it. Add lemon peel and vanilla extract. Beat the egg white until it is stiff. Add a pinch of salt and mix it into the millet. Heat up the shortening in a coated frying pan, put the mixture into it, and distribute the berries on the surface. Let it thicken at

Roast the millet in a small pot until it begins to have a nice aroma. Add the vegetable broth. Let it boil, then simmer for 30 minutes at low heat. Then let it absorb more moisture afterwards. Wash the leek thoroughly and cut it into ½-inch wide strips. Heat up the shortening in a frying pan. Stew the leek in it and then add the cooked broccoli and millet. Pour the vegetable broth over this. Flavor with salt, cayenne pepper, and grated nutmeg. Before serving, stir in crème fraîche and lemon juice.

■ Anti-cellulite active agents: Potassium, silicon, zinc, copper, fiber

Tip: Cook the broccoli together with the vegetables for the "Broccoli salad" cold snack (page 101) and store it covered in the refrigerator.

BARLEY PATTY WITH PEPPER SALAD

½ pint vegetable broth (ready made), 3 ounces barley grains, 1 onion, 1 teaspoon shortening, parsley, salt, pepper, paprika, 2 teaspoons shortening, 1 red pepper, 1 teaspoon oil, 1 tablespoon vinegar, salt, pepper, and as much chives as you like

Bring the broth to a boil. Sprinkle the barley into it and let it simmer at low heat for 10 minutes, covered. Then remove it from the stove and let it absorb more moisture for about 15 minutes. Cut the onion into small pieces, fry it in the shortening until it is golden brown, and then add it to the barley paste. Season with the herbs and spices. Form three patties with your hands wet and fry the patties in the shortening (two patties for the evening, one for

the "Barley burger" cold snack; see page 100). Clean the pepper and cut it into thin strips. Mix it with the dressing of oil, vinegar, salt, pepper, and chives.

■ Anti-cellulite active agents: Potassium, silicon, zinc, selenium, fiber

ow temperature until the surface is dry.

Anti-cellulite active agents: Silicon, opper, fiber

ip 1: Instead of raspberries, you can se sour cherries, apricots, or apples.

ip 2: You can buy vanilla extract made f real vanilla from heath-food stores.

CHINESE VEGETABLES WITH MUSHROOMS

3½ ounces beef, 1 carrot, ½ rod of leek, 7 ounces mushrooms, 1 teaspoon shortening, salt, pepper, ½ cup vegetable broth (ready made), 1 clove garlic, soy sauce, powdered ginger, pepper

Cut the beef and carrot into thin strips. Cut the leek into ½-inch wide strips and slice up the mushrooms. Heat up the shortening in a coated frying pan. Brown the meat briefly and then flavor with salt and pepper. Remove from frying pan. Put the vegetables and mushrooms into the pan and fry. Add vegetable broth. Stir the vegetables until firm but not too soft. Add the meat again and season with the chopped up clove of garlic, soy sauce, powdered ginger, and pepper.

■ Anti-cellulite active agents: Potassium, copper, zinc, selenium, fiber

Tip: You can easily substitute the beef with turkey or tofu.

POTATO TORTILLA

9 ounces potatoes, 1 onion, salt, pepper, 1 tablespoon shortening, 1 egg, 3 tablespoons skim milk (1% fat), as much chives as you like

Cook the potatoes with their skins on, let them cool off, and cut them into slices. Cut the onion into cubes and mix them with the potatoes. Add salt and pepper. Heat up the shortening in a coated frying pan, add the potatoes and onions and fry them, stirring occasionally. Whisk the egg with the milk and pour it over the potatoes. Fry the tortilla at medium heat for 5 minutes, covered. Glide it onto a plate and sprinkle it with chives.

■ Anti-cellulite active agents: Potassium, copper, fiber

Tip 1: Cook enough potatoes so that you can have them for a cold lunch snack for the next day (e.g., "Radishes and potato salad," see page 100). This saves time and energy.

Tip 2: Buy potatoes that remain firm when cooked. They do not fall apart as easily.

MILLET PANCAKE WITH SPINACH

1 tablespoon millet flour, 1 egg, 4 tablespoons mineral water, salt, 7 ounces fresh spinach, 1½ ounces sour cream (low fat), 2 tablespoons grated parmesan cheese, 1 clove garlic, grated nutmeg, salt, pepper, 1 teaspoon butter, 1 teaspoon flour,

MUSHROOM STEAK WITH FIELD LETTUCE

5 ounces mushrooms, 1 onion, 1 teaspoon shortening, salt, pepper, 1 egg, 2 tablespoons whole-grain bread crumbs, as much parsley as you like, lemon juice, 1 tablespoon shortening, 2 ounces field lettuce or spinach, 2 ounces kefir, 2 tablespoons lemon juice, salt, pepper

Clean the mushrooms and cut them into thin slices. Finely chop the onions and fry them in heated shortening. Add the mushrooms and cook them until they are soft. Season with salt and pepper. Let them cool. Mix the egg and whole-grain bread crumbs together well. Combine them with the mushrooms and onions. Flavor with parsley, salt, pepper, and lemon juice. Make three patties with your hands wet and fry the patties in hot

shortening at medium to low heat until they are golden brown. Clean the field lettuce. Prepare a sauce from kefir, lemon juice, salt, and pepper. Pour it over the salad.

■ Anti-cellulite active agents: Potassium, selenium, fiber

SAUERKRAUT QUICHE

1 ounce flour, salt, 2 tablespoons butter, ice water, 1 small onion, 1 teaspoon shortening, ½ egg, 3 ounces skim milk (1% fat), 3½ ounces sauerkraut, ½ apple, caraway seeds, salt, pepper, 1 slice turkey breast

Mix the flour, salt, and butter. Break the mixture up with your hands until it resembles fine bread crumbs. Add enough water so that you make a soft but not sticky dough. Chill it in the refrigerator. Finely chop the onion and fry it in heated shortening until it is golden brown. Whisk the egg with the milk and add salt and pepper. Roll out the dough until it is very thin and can cover a small pie pan. Cut the sauerkraut and apple into small pieces. Add caraway seeds, salt, and pepper. Spread this out with the onions on the

3 ounces skim milk (1% fat), lemon juice, 1 teaspoon shortening

Make a dough with the millet flour, egg, mineral water, and a pinch of salt. Let it sit for about 20 minutes. Lightly cook the spinach in a hot pan. Press out the excess water and chop the spinach coarsely. Mix it with the sour cream, parmesan, chopped clove of garlic, nutmeg, salt, and pepper. For a white sauce, melt the butter in a small pot, dust it with flour, and slowly pour milk over it. Add to it salt, pepper, and lemon juice. Let the shortening become hot in a coated frying pan. Fry two pancakes, fill them with spinach, and fold them up. Pour the white sauce over them.

■ Anti-cellulite active agents: Potassium, silicon, copper, fiber

UNPEELED POTATOES WITH TOMATOES

9 ounces unpeeled potatoes, 5¼ ounces cottage cheese (low fat), garlic, plenty of chopped herbs (e.g., chives, parsley, dill, pimpernel, lemon-balm mint, thyme, tarragon), salt, pepper, lemon juice, 3 small tomatoes

Cook the potatoes in a little water. Mince the garlic and mix it with the potatoes and the finely chopped herbs. Add salt, pepper, and lemon juice. Slice up the tomatoes and serve them together with the potatoes and cottage cheese on a plate.

■ Anti-cellulite active agents: Potassium, copper, fiber

Tip 1: Cook enough potatoes (about 23 ounces) so that you can also make a salad (see page 100) and a tortilla (see page 106). Make the salad while the potatoes are still warm. Store the unpeeled potatoes for the tortilla in the refrigerator.

Tip 2: Herbs can be easily grown in a garden or even in a pot along a windowsill.

dough. Cut the turkey breast into strips and place them on top of it. Pour the egg/milk mixture over it. Bake the quiche in a preheated oven at 390° for 20 minutes and then at 350° for another 10 minutes.

■ Anti-cellulite active agents: Potassium, copper, fiber

FISH WITH SPINACH

9 ounces fresh spinach, 1 onion, 1 teaspoon shortening, 9-ounce codfish cutlet, 1 lemon or lime, salt, pepper, grated nutmeg, 2 teaspoons crème fraîche

Wash and clean the spinach. Cook it in salted water for 1 minute. Pour it through a strainer, squeeze out the excess water from the spinach, and chop it coarsely. Dice the onion and fry it in hot shortening in a coated frying pan. Add the spinach and briefly stir. Wash the fish, dab it dry, sprinkle some lemon juice over it, add salt and pepper, and place it on the spinach. Let it cook for 6 to 8 minutes, or until it is done, with the lid on. Take the cod out. Mix the spinach with salt, pepper, grated nutmeg, and crème fraîche. Serve

with the fish and lemon or lime slices.

■ Anti-cellulite active agents: Potassium, selenium

Tip: If it is not the season for fresh spinach, you can buy it frozen in the supermarket.

It is not necessary to have power food for breakfast. Here are six recipes for you to choose from.

Why you should have breakfast especially during a diet:

■ <u>Because, if you don't, you will not do things as well and you will be doubly hungry at noon</u>. If you really cannot eat anything in the morning, take your breakfast to work and eat it during a break.

■ <u>You can choose from six types of breakfasts presented</u>. Eat what you feel like eating the most, but alternate as often as possible.

Eating breakfast so that you have energy in the morning.

■ <u>You can drink</u> coffee with a little milk, black tea, herbal tea, or fruit tea as much as you like.

■ <u>Tip</u>: Try to eat fruits that are in season. The only exception is bananas, which are one of the power foods.

300-CALORIE BREAKFASTS

BANANA-MILLET YOGURT

*5 ounces yogurt (1% fat),
3 tablespoons millet flakes, 1 teaspoo
lemon juice, 1 teaspoon honey,
1 banana, lemon-balm mint*

Mix the yogurt, millet flakes, lemo
juice, and honey. Cut the banana int
slices and add it on top. Garnish wit
some lemon-balm mint leaves.
Tip: Prepare only shortly befor
breakfast, because the millet flake
get too soft otherwise.

UNDAY BREAKFAST

egg, 1 teaspoon butter, 2 slices whole-
rain toast, chives, 2 pickles, 1 glass
 ounces) fruit juice

ry the egg in a coated frying pan with
alf of the butter. Spread the remain-
g butter on one slice of whole-grain
ast and cover it with chopped chives.
ut the fried egg, sunny-side up, and
he pickles onto the other slice of
ast. Drink a glass of fruit juice with it
preferably fresh).

CRUNCHY CURRANT MUESLI

*1 teaspoon butter, 2 teaspoons barley
flakes, 1 teaspoon sunflower seeds,
1 teaspoon honey, 4½ ounces sour milk
or buttermilk (1% fat), 3½ ounces
currants, 1 teaspoon raisins*
Heat up the butter in a coated frying pan.
Add the barley flakes, sunflower seeds,
and honey. Fry them until they are golden
brown. Mix the sour milk/buttermilk with
currants and the cooled flakes. Sprinkle
raisins on top.

HONEY SOUR CREAM ROLL

*1 whole-grain roll, 2 ounces sour cream
(low fat), 1 teaspoon honey, 1 orange*

Cut open the roll. Spread with sour
cream. Add some honey over it. Have
an orange with it.
Tip: Instead of honey, you can also
have marmalade or fruit preserves
(e.g., 2 ounces pureed strawberries,
mixed with 1 teaspoon honey and
vanilla extract).

APPLE COTTAGE CHEESE

*4½ ounces cottage cheese, 2 table-
spoons milk, 1 apple, 1 teaspoon
lemon juice, cinnamon powder, 1
teaspoon honey, 1 whole wheat
cracker*

Stir the cottage cheese with milk until
it is creamy. Slice up the apple, sprinkle some lemon juice over it, and mix
it into the cottage cheese. Add honey
and ground cinnamon. Eat it with a
whole wheat cracker.

HAM SANDWICH WITH MELON

*1 slice whole-grain bread, 2 teaspoons
butter, 4 slices smoked ham,
¼ honeydew melon*

Spread butter on the whole-grain
bread and cover it with smoked ham.
Eat the honeydew melon with it.
Tip: You can substitute the ham with 1
slice of cheese, regular ham, or turkey
breast.

100-CALORIE EXTRAS

You can have these small extras in between meals if you're hungry.

Twice a day, you can and even should nibble on something. That will keep your blood sugar level up and your hunger away. You have the choice between some sweets or hearty snacks that are 100 calories each. Always have only your daily ration on hand so that you won't weaken and go for the cakes, cookies, etc.

A crunchy apple: A perfect in-between meal snack

BANANA, ETC.

A banana, all by itself, is an ideal in-between-meal snack because it is a power food with a high potassium content. You can buy it, take it with you, and eat it anytime, anywhere. A nice ripe banana has 100 calories (see more about bananas on page 96).

Banana variations:

■ Cut a small banana and kiwi into small pieces and sprinkle some lemon juice over them.

■ Fry a small banana in a coated frying pan with 1 teaspoon butter until it is golden brown. Sprinkle 1 teaspoon of grated coconut over it.

Other 100-calorie fruits you can eat as well: 1 large apple; 4 apricots; 1 pear; 1 grapefruit; 2 kiwis; 5 tangerines; 2 nectarines; 1 orange; 2 peaches; 10 plums; 5 ounces pineapple, yellow plums, or grapes; 7 ounces blackberries, currants, gooseberries, cherries, or honeydew melon; 10½ ounces strawberries, raspberries or watermelon.

SANDWICH

If you need something more substantial, you can have a 100-calorie sandwich with whole-grain bread, because that will give you extra active agents like zinc, copper, iron, magnesium, and fiber. In addition to that, whole grain has less calories and keeps you full longer. You have, as a choice:

■ Honey roll: ½ whole-grain roll with 1 teaspoon butter and 1 teaspoon honey.

■ Marmalade zwieback: 1 whole-grain zwieback with 1 teaspoon crème fraîche and 1 teaspoon marmalade.

■ Nut cracker: 1 whole wheat cracker with 1 tablespoon nut butter.

■ Chive sandwich: ½ slice whole-grain bread with 1 teaspoon butter and a lot of chopped chives.

If you don't use a spread, there is even more to chew for 100 calories: 1 whole-grain roll; 1 slice of whole-grain bread; 3 rice cakes; 3 whole wheat crackers; 2 slices zwieback.

SPICY FOOD

There are many salty power foods that have 100 calories. Especially good are sauerkraut and unpeeled potatoes.

■ Chop 5 ounces raw sauerkraut and ½ apple into small pieces. Mix them together and sprinkle 1 teaspoon hazelnuts over them.

■ Chop 5 ounces sauerkraut and ¼ onion into small pieces. Mix with 1 teaspoon oil and a pinch of caraway seeds.

■ Put 1 teaspoon crème fraîche over a medium-sized unpeeled potato. Sprinkle with salt, pepper, paprika, and fresh herbs.

■ Cut one large, hot, unpeeled potato in half and let 1 teaspoon butter melt on it. Flavor with a lot of herbs and a little salt.

■ Put a slice (1 ounce) mozzarella and a basil leaf on each of two large slices of tomatoes. Add a lot of pepper and a little salt.

For finger foods, you can have cucumber (28 ounces), kohlrabi (14 ounces), carrots (12 ounces), peppers (17½ ounces), or tomatoes (21 ounces).

MILK PRODUCTS

It is important to use only pure milk products—without heat treatment, sugar, flavoring, fruits, and other additives.

■ Energy drink: Blend 3 ounces kefir, orange juice, and some vanilla extract in a mixer set at the highest level.

■ Sour cream mix: Stir 2½ ounces sour cream (or quark), 2 tablespoons mineral water, and 1 teaspoon honey until it is creamy. Add 1 teaspoon cocoa powder (or cinnamon, lemon juice, orange juice, or vanilla extra—a little of each).

■ Fruity milk: Mix 4½ ounces sour milk or buttermilk (1% fat) with 3½ ounces strawberries, raspberries, or other berries/fruits.

■ Honey yogurt: Mix 5 ounces lowfat yogurt with 1 teaspoon honey.

Other pure milk products that are about 100 calories: 5 ounces yogurt (low fat); 6 ounces sour milk or buttermilk (1% fat); 4½ ounces kefir (low fat); 4½ ounces whole milk.

COFFEE AND SWEETS

Eating sweets gives you a lift (see page 97) and, as long as you don't eat too much of them, there isn't much fat. So go ahead and nibble something sweet with your afternoon coffee or tea. In moderation, you can certainly enjoy eating something "unhealthy."

Coffee and tea have no calories. So you can drink as much as you like. But do not add sugar (or a sweetening agent, see page 97). You can add 3 tablespoons of regular milk with your first cup of coffee or tea.

■ As for pastries, you can have the following: 2 butter cookies; 4 whole-grain cookies; 1 small piece of fruit cake with biscuit dough; 1 piece of biscuit roll filled with marmalade; 5 spoon-shaped biscuits.

■ Here are some other 100-calorie extras that you can nibble on: 5 fruit candies; 2 cream toffees; 15 gummy bears; 4 pieces of chocolate; 2 pralines; 1 large scoop of ice cream; 2 ounces of popcorn; 4 marzipan "potatoes."

WHAT TO DRINK?

You need to drink a lot to cleanse out your body.

Fat reduction produces a substance called keton, which is expelled via the kidney and leads to the body losing fluid. Therefore, you must drink a lot during a diet. That is especially so when you exercise at the same time. Otherwise, your body becomes dehydrated. You can develop a headache, a decrease in performance, and a general sense of discomfort.

Herbal tea for the body.

WATER

Drink as much water as you can. It is best to alternate between:
- mineral water (from natural or artificial springs)
- spring water (no carbonation)
- tap water (if the amount of nitrate, lead, and chlorine is safe)
- bottled water.
- Normal water tastes like mineral water if you use a water filter.
- Medicinal water should be drunk only for healing purposes, because of its specific mineral content.

When you buy mineral water, pay attention to the analysis values. It should contain as little sodium as possible (at the most 10 mg per liter). Whether or not it's carbonated does not matter.

Tip: For a change, flavor the water with a bit of orange or lemon juice.

HERBAL TEA

Drinking herbal teas is recommended during a cellulite diet (and at most 2 weeks afterwards). The herbs are strong cleansers. Try this recipe: Pour ¼ liter boiling water into a glass containing 1 teaspoon each of stinging nettle, birch leaves, and horsetail. Let it sit for 10 minutes and then pour it into a thermos. Drink it throughout the day in small sips (and at best before meals). You can also prepare the tea with only one of the three herbs and alternate daily.
- Herbal teas from blackberry, strawberry, or raspberry leaves and hawthorn, apple, lemon, or orange skins help quench your thirst. If you want, you can also add such healing herbs as mallow, peppermint, balm-mint, aniseed, or fennel. How much you put in depends on how strong you want it to taste.

Tip: Fruit teas taste especially good cold and with a lemon slice.

COFFEE & TEA

You can certainly have coffee and tea during your diet, but they will not quench you thirst. If you drink too much of them, the excess caffeine will make you nervous and restless, and may even cause your muscles to tremble. Besides, an overdose of coffee or tea flushes out valuable minerals from the body.

■ You can have <u>three cups</u> of coffee or black tea during the day. It will wake you up and increase your alertness.

■ <u>Black tea</u> is better for the stomach than coffee. Its tannin calms the mucous membrane of the stomach and intestine.

Important: Drink coffee and tea, if possible, without sugar but with 3 tablespoons of fresh milk per cup at the most. Sugar has 20 calories per cup. Sweetening agents are not recommended (see page 97).

Tip: If you lack iron, drink coffee and tea only an hour after a meal, because it hinders the absorption of iron into the blood.

JUICE

<u>Fermented sauerkraut juice</u> helps cleanse the connective tissue. It is available in select health-food or natural-food stores. If you can find it, drink a glass (3 ounces) daily before breakfast or in-between meals. Other fruit and vegetable juices are also good thirst quenchers during a diet. They are easier to find and supply the body with minerals. Sweet juices, however, have more calories.

■ <u>The best juices</u> are those freshly squeezed from citrus fruits, carrots, apples, radishes, and cucumbers.

■ If you buy juice from a store make sure it is 100% juice, without additives.

■ Nectar fruit juices, concentrated fruit juice beverages, lemonades, cola beverages, and vegetable drinks (with only 40% vegetable juice) are not suitable.

Tip: If you mix sweet fruit juices with water, you will have fewer calories and less of an increase in your blood sugar level.

ALCOHOL

In principle, there is nothing wrong with a glass of wine or champagne now and then in the evening—assuming that it really is just one glass. It should be an absolutely dry brand. But alcohol in any form during a diet is always a trap, because it stimulates the appetite and makes it harder to eat moderately. Alcohol also contains plenty of calories: 75 calories in a glass of dry white wine to 180 calories in a cocktail. These are empty calories for the body, because they do not offer anything in terms of nutrition.

If you want to go on a cellulite diet, you can follow this 10-day plan. Every day you have a power food at least twice.

DIET PLAN

Days 1–5	Breakfast	Snack
Monday	Honey sour cream roll (page 109)	1 large banana
Tuesday	Banana-millet yogurt (page 108)	Chive sandwich (page 110)
Wednesday	Ham sandwich with melon (page 109)	1 large banana
Thursday	Apple cottage cheese (page 108)	Nut cracker (page 110)
Friday	Banana-millet yogurt (page 108)	5 ounces pineapple

"... at 6 o'clock at the gym? Perfect!"

Lunch	Snack	Dinner	Shopping list/ingredients
Sauerkraut with grapes (page 102)	Carrots (up to 10 ounces)	Unpeeled potatoes with tomatoes (page 107)	7 ounces sour cream (low fat), 9 ounces potatoes, 10½ ounces carrots, 5 ounces fresh sauerkraut, 3 tomatoes, chives, parsley, dill, 1 large banana, 1 orange, 3 ounces purple grapes, 2 whole-grain rolls
Radish and potato salad (page 100)	1–2 kohlrabi	Millet pancake with spinach (page 106)	3 ounces milk (1% fat), 1½ ounces sour cream (low fat), 5 ounces yogurt (1% fat), 2 tablespoons parmesan cheese, 2 eggs, 5 ounces potatoes, 1–2 kohlrabi, a bunch of radishes, 7 ounces spinach, chives, cress, 1 small banana, ½ whole-grain roll, 1 tablespoon millet flour, 1 ounce millet flakes
Mushroooms with field lettuce (page 103)	Honey roll (page 110)	Barley patty with pepper salad (page 105)	4 slices smoked ham, 3½ ounces mushrooms, 2 ounces field lettuce/spinach, 1 kohlrabi, 1 red pepper, chives, parsley, 1 large banana, ¼ honeydew melon, 1 slice whole-grain bread, ½ whole-grain roll, 3 ounces barley grains
Barley burger (page 100)	Tomatoes with mozzarella (page 111)	Potato tortilla (page 106)	½ ounce milk (1% fat), 4½ ounces cottage cheese, 1 ounce mozzarella, 1 egg, 9 ounces potatoes, some lettuce leaves, 2 tomatoes, chives, 1 apple, 1 whole-grain roll
Millet cream with fruit (page 102)	Potato with butter (page 111)	Fish with spinach (page 107)	9-ounce codfish cutlet, 4½ ounces milk (1% fat), 5 ounces yogurt (1% fat), 2 teaspoons crème fraîche, 3½ ounces potatoes, 9 ounces spinach, 5 ounces pineapple, 1 banana, 9 ounces seasonal fruit, .7 ounce millet flour, 1 ounce millet flakes

*Having a friend join
you on a diet is
more fun and provides
more support*

Days 6–10	Breakfast	Snack
Saturday	Crunchy currant muesli (page 109)	Unpeeled potatoes with crème fraîche (page 111)
Sunday	Sunday breakfast (page 108)	Energy drink (page 111)
Monday	Banana-millet yogurt (page 108)	Sauerkraut and apple salad (page 111)
Tuesday	Marmalade sour cream roll (instead of honey; page 109)	Cucumber salad (up to 28 ounces)
Wednesday	Apple cottage cheese (page 108)	1 large banana

Lunch	Snack	Dinner	Shopping list/ingredients
Spinach with chicken breast (page 103)	Fried banana with coconut (page 110)	Mushroom steak with field lettuce (page 106)	3 ounces chicken breast fillet, 4½ ounces sour milk or buttermilk (1% fat), 2 ounces kefir (low fat), .7 ounce crème fraîche, 1 egg, 5 ounces mushrooms, 2 ounces field lettuce/spinach, 1 carrot, 3½ ounces potatoes, 2 ounces fresh spinach, parsley, 1 small banana, 3½ ounces currants, 1 slice whole-grain bread, .7 ounce barley flakes
Stuffed avocado (page 101)	Coffee with 2 butter cookies (page 111)	Chinese vegetables with mushrooms (page 105)	3½ ounces beef, 1 ounce milk (1% fat), 3 ounces kefir (1% fat), 1 egg, 2 ounces watercress, 9 ounces mushrooms, 1 carrot (3½ ounces), ½ rod of leek, chives, ½ avocado, 1 orange, 2 slices whole-grain toast
Broccoli salad (page 101)	¼ honeydew melon	Sweet millet with raspberries (page 104)	4½ ounces milk (1% fat), 5 ounces yogurt (1% fat), 1 egg, 9 ounces broccoli, 5 ounces fresh sauerkraut, ½ apple, 1 small banana, 5 ounces raspberries, ¼ honeydew melon, 1 slice whole-grain bread, 1½ ounce millet, 1 ounce millet flakes
Avocado with yogurt sauce (page 102)	Banana-kiwi salad (page 110)	Sauerkraut quiche (page 106)	1 slice turkey breast, 3 ounces milk (1% fat), 2 ounces sour cream (low fat), 3½ ounces yogurt (1% fat), ½ ounce crème fraîche, ½ egg; 28 ounces cucumber salad, 3½ ounces fresh sauerkraut, ½ avocado, 1 tomato, parsley, ½ apple, 1 small banana, 1 kiwi, 1 orange, 1 whole grain roll
Barley cookies with cucumber (page 102)	Sauerkraut-onion salad (page 111)	Stir fried millet and broccoli (page 104)	½ ounce milk (1% fat), 1½ ounce yogurt (1% fat), 4½ ounces cottage cheese (low fat), 1½ ounce crème fraîche, ½ egg, 7 ounces broccoli, ½ rod of leek, 3½ ounces cucumber salad, 5 ounces fresh sauerkraut, dill, 1 banana, 9 ounces seasonal fruit, 1 ounce barley, 1½ ounce millet

SHOPPING LIST

Here is a shopping list of what you'll need if you follow the 10-day diet plan.

Copy these two pages and take them with you when you go food shopping.

The first shopping list contains, among other things, grains. You won't need to use up the amounts given during the 10-day diet, but grains and flakes last for about a year when they are stored in a dry place (preferably in a sealed glass jar).

Important: Buy fresh and, if possible, organically-grown produce.

WHAT YOU SHOULD HAVE AT HOME

FATS
Butter
Melted butter or coconut oil
Olive oil (cold pressed)
Sunflower oil (cold pressed)

HERBS & SPICES
Salt
Mustard
Fruit or wine vinegar
Balsamic vinegar (optional)
Soy sauce
Fresh herbs (basil, estragon, lemon-balm mint)
Garlic
Peppercorns for grinding (black and white)
Paprika powder
Curry powder
Ginger powder
Caraway seeds
Thyme
Nutmeg
Vanilla extract
Cinnamon powder

FRUITS & VEGETABLES
Lemons, untreated
Onions

BEVERAGES
Mineral water

(a case)
1 bottle apple juice (natural)
1 bottle multi-vitamin juice
Coffee/black tea
Herbal tea
Fruit tea

OTHER
Whole wheat crackers
Flour
whole-grain breadcrumbs
Oats (coarse)
Hazelnuts (whole)
Walnuts
Marmalade
Maple syrup
Honey
Coconut flakes
Sunflower seeds
Pine nuts
Raisins
Nut butter
Vegetable broth
Butter cookies
Sour cucumber/ pickles (cornichons)

SHOPPING LIST #1
for Monday, Tuesday, Wednesday of Week 1

POWER FOOD
17½ ounces millet (grind 1 ounce)
17½ ounces millet flakes
17½ ounces barley (grind 3 ounces)
17½ ounces barley flakes
30 ounces potatoes
5 ounces sauerkraut
7 ounces spinach
3½ ounces mushrooms
3 bananas

MILK/MILK PRODUCTS
1 pint milk (1% fat)
9 ounces sour cream (low fat)
5 ounces yogurt (1% fat)
1 container crème fraîche
.7 ounce parmesan cheese

MEAT/FISH/EGGS
7 eggs (for the entire diet)
4 slices smoked ham

VEGETABLE/FRUIT
2 ounces field lettuce or young spinach
17½ ounces carrots
1 red pepper
3 kohlrabi
a bunch of radishes
a small package of cress
a bunch each of dill, parsley, chives
3 tomatoes
1 honeydew melon
3 oranges (also for later)
Purple grapes (at least 3 ounces)

BREAD
1 loaf whole-grain bread
3 whole-grain rolls

SHOPPING LIST #2
for Thursday, Friday, Saturday, Sunday of Week 1

POWER FOOD
14 ounces mushrooms
10½ ounces spinach
1 avocado
2 bananas

MILK/MILK PRODUCTS
1 pint milk (1% fat)
5 ounces yogurt (1% fat)
4½ ounces sour milk or buttermilk (1% fat)
4½ ounces cottage cheese (low fat)
4½ ounces kefir (low fat)
Mozzarella (at least 1 ounce)

MEAT/FISH/EGGS
9 ounces codfish cutlet
3 ounces chicken breast fillet
3½ ounces beef (chuck or round)

VEGETABLE/FRUIT
2 ounces cress
2 ounces field lettuce or young spinach
1 rod of leek
a head of lettuce
a bunch of parsley and chives
2 tomatoes
1 pineapple
1 apple
3½ ounces currants or other berries (may be frozen)

BREAD
1 whole-grain roll
1 package of whole-grain bread

SHOPPING LIST #3
for Monday, Tuesday, Wednesday of Week 2

POWER FOOD
16 ounces broccoli
14 ounces fresh sauerkraut
3 small bananas

MILK/MILK PRODUCTS
½ pint milk (1% fat)
2 ounces sour cream (low fat)
4½ ounces cottage cheese
10½ ounces yogurt (1% fat)

MEAT/FISH/EGGS
1 slice turkey breast (.7 ounce)

VEGETABLE/FRUIT
2 cucumber salad
1 tomato
a bunch of dill
1 apple
5 ounces raspberries (may be frozen)
1 kiwi

BREAD
1 whole-grain roll

STICKING WITH IT!

Learn how to motivate yourself again and again so that you really can achieve your goal.

Now you know all the things that you can do to firm up your figure and specifically the problem zones around your posterior and hips. But you may ask yourself: How can I fit all this into the course of an already full day? And even if I succeed, how can I keep myself motivated to stick with it through anti-cellulite products, exercise, dieting?

For that, we have the weekly planners for applying anti-cellulite products, exercising, and diet. It would be better if you made up your own personal daily plan so that you can realistically organize your personal care and exercise activities. But do not overdo it! Begin with an easier plan so that when you have established a routine, you can progressively add more to it. The feeling of having stuck with it and of having had success is the best motivation for you to continue.

Say to yourself "I am beautiful, slim, and firm!"

Begin at the right time

Don't begin your problem zone activities when you are under a lot of stress. Changing jobs, moving to a new place, personal problems, or trouble at work are certainly not the right circumstances.

Visualizing in a meditative posture: Good if you can sit this way longer.

Begin when your life is calm and you are mentally ready to make the commitment. That will enhance the chances for success. The best time to start is after menstruation.

Don't be dissuaded

Once you begin your cellulite plan, there will be many temptations to break it. Being invited to see a movie may clash with your exercise schedule. Comparing what you're eating to what others are eating may make it hard for you to stick with what's on your plate. Some people may even tell you that you can't do it and to give up. These are the times when you need to be especially determined. Remember that many times discouraging comments mask envy—that you are doing it, and they're not. There will always be another movie showing that is more convenient for you. There is always that in-between-meals snack that's in your plan. The fact that you are taking better care of your body does not mean that you are giving up your life. As a matter of fact, you are enhancing your life. You will be more confident about how you look and you will feel physically better because of the wonderful shape that you're in.

Do it for yourself!

Before you begin your problem zone program, think about why you are doing this and who are you doing this for.

The right reasons:

■ I want to keep my good figure.

■ I want to make my body the best that it can be.

■ I want to remove the tissue sludge and smooth out the cellulite areas of my body.

■ I want to firm up my body and improve its condition.

■ I want to feel good about my body, feel more beautiful and energetic. I simply want to be in better shape.

The wrong reasons:

■ My partner does not like my figure.

■ I want a figure that attracts other people.

■ I hate my body because it is completely different from what I want it to be.

■ I have a heavy build, but I want to become just as slim as my friend.

■ I have trouble making friends because my body is so ugly.

Program your subconscious!

Good intentions are often not sufficient if you really want to lead a different life. Although action may seem to be propelled only from your mind, it also comes from the center of your feelings and, thus, for the most part from your subconscious. Try the following technique.

Visualization exercise: My body is beautiful, slim, and firm.

Find a quiet place in which you will not be disturbed. Close your eyes and imagine that you are going down a flight of stairs. As you go down each step, you are going deeper into yourself. Then, in your mind, open the door to a small, quiet room that contains nothing but a large mirror with a blue frame and a large white screen. You see in the mirror the image of your naked body, the way it still looks at this moment. Wipe this image away with a decisive movement or, even better, smash the mirror! Now you turn to the screen. There, your body appears in front of your spiritual eye as you want it to be. Imagine with pleasure all the details: the tight upper thighs, the flat stomach, the tight buttocks, the smooth skin, and so on. Remain for at least 10 minutes in this state. Do not consider this as a chore, enjoy it! Then, in your thoughts, you leave the room and slowly climb up the stairs. As you climb further up, breathe deeply and open your eyes. Repeat this mental exercise every day, preferably before you go to sleep. It will help you to change the negative motives for getting rid of the excess fat and sagging muscles into positive feelings towards your body. Because it is through self-love and enhanced self-confidence, not self-deprecation, that you will succeed in getting rid of your problem zones.

With all this going on, you should not forget that if you want energy, you must also rest.

Calories at a Glance

Calories	Breakfast	Main meal	Snack	Sweet/Salty food	Beverage
25 cal	Honey 1 tsp Condensed milk 1 tbsp Candied fruit 1 tsp Sugar 1 tsp Cottage cheese 1 tbsp	Cauliflower 3½ oz Mushrooms 3½ oz Chicory 2 Ketchup 1 tbsp Leek 3½ oz Pepper 1	Apricot 1 Mixed pickles 2 oz Radishes 1 bh Tomatoes 2	Fruit drop 1 Chewing gum 3 Drop biscuit 1 Waffle rolls 1	Liqueur 1 gl Tea w/ sugar cup
50 cal	Butter/margarine 1 tsp Whole wheat cracker 1 Nut-nougat creme 1 tsp Turkey breast, sm. 1½ sl Melted cheese .7 oz	Meat gravy 6 tbsp Kohlrabi 7 oz Parmesan cheese 1 tbsp Sour cream 2 tbsp Tomato sauce 4 tbsp Zucchini 2	Kiwi 1 Green olives 10 Orange 1 Peach 1	Peanut candies 12 Praline 1 Caramel 2 Dried plums 3	Cappuccino cup Coffee w/ milk cup Brandy 1 gl
75 cal	Ham 1 sl Edam cheese (low fat) 1 sl Boiled egg 1 Cream cheese (low fat) 1 tbsp Cheese 1 sl Cooked ham 1 sl	Green beans 7 oz Créme fraîche 1 tbsp Lettuce w/ yogurt p Shellfish 3½ oz Bread crumbs 1 tbsp	Apple 1 Pear 1 Strawberries 7 oz Grapefruit 1	Raisins 2 tbsp Cream, sweetened 1 tbsp Salted almonds 7	Buttermilk gl Coffee w/ milk & sugar cup Tonic water 3 oz
100 cal	Swiss cheese 1 sl Creamy fresh cheese 1 oz Parma ham 2 sl Uncooked ham 1½ sl Sunny-side up egg 1 Whole-grain bread 1 sl	Melted butter 1 tbsp Peas p Lettuce w/ oil p Lox, sm 2 oz Scampi 3½ oz Cooked spinach p	Bouillon w/ egg p Fruit yogurt 3½ oz Hazelnuts 10 Carrots 4 Banana 1	Sherbet scoop 1 Cookies 10 Chocolate 7 oz Whole-grain cookies 4 Chocolate fudge 1 Biscuit roll 1	Apple juice gl Beer, light 3 oz Bitter lemon 4 oz
150 cal	Roll 1 Gouda 1½ sl Sweet roll 1 Liverwurst 1 oz Whole-grain roll 1	Hollandaise sauce 4 tbsp Mayonnaise 1 tbsp Brussels sprouts, ck p Peeled potatoes, ck 7 oz Tomato salad p	Mango 1 Rollmops 1 Grapes 7 oz	Chocolate danish 1 Crêpe 1 Fruit cocktail p Ice cream scoop 1	Whole milk 7½ oz Wine, red/white 7½ oz
200 cal	Croissant 1 Cold cut salad 2 oz Cheese toast 1 Scrambled eggs 2 Cornflakes w/ milk p	Chicken, fr p Turkey cutlet, fr p Veal cutlet, fr p Rice, ck p Wiener sausages 2 Onion soup p	Melon w/ ham p Fruit salad p Cream cheese (low fat) 4½ oz Onion shortcake 1 sl	Danish 1 Fruit cake 1 Vanilla custard p Waffle, bk 1	Cocoa 7½ oz Sweet champagne 5½ oz Dry champagne 7½ oz Ice coffee gl
250 cal	Muesli w/ milk p Omelet p Salami sandwich 1 Tee sausage 2 oz Honey roll 1	Hamburger 1 Noodles, ck p Pork chop p Cream of tomato soup p	Yogurt-fruit soup p Trail mix 2 oz Dried fruit 3½ oz	Apple turnover 1 Caramel cream p Madeira cake 1 pc Cream tart 1	Beer w/ lemon 15 oz
300 cal	Croissant w/ marmalade 1 Ham and egg p Cheese roll 1	Calf liver, fr p Potatoes, fr p Greek salad p Noodles in cream sauce p Pepper steak p Red perch fillet, fr p	Avocado 1 Spring roll 1 Crab cocktail p Pizza ½	Florentine 1 Chocolate mousse p Cheesecake 2 oz Jello w/ milk p Crumb cake 1 pc	Fruit punch 9 oz Malt beer 15 oz
350 cal	Bacon 2 oz Liverwurst roll 1 Egg pancake 2 pc	Sausage 1 Fried chicken ½ Blue trout p Goulash p Potato salad w/ mayo p French fries 5 oz	Pastry w/ stew p Hawaiian toast p	Gummy bears 3½ oz Fruit cake w/ cream 1 pc Popcorn, buttered 3½ oz Licorice 3½ oz	Fruit shake 9 oz Mikshake 9 oz Chocolate shake gl
400–500 cal	Sunny-side up eggs w/ bacon 2	Freshwater trout filet p Veal cacciatore p Veal cutlet p Roast lamb p Roast pork w/ gravy p Breaded veal cutlet p	Camembert cheese p	Buttercream tart 1 pc Chips 2½ oz Ice cream w/ topping p Salted peanuts 2½ oz Pretzel sticks 3½ oz	

Abbreviations

bh	= bunch	cup	= 4 oz. cup	p	= medium portion	sm	= smoked
bk	= baked	fr	= fried	pc	= piece	tbsp	= tablespoon
ck	= cooked	gl	= 6 oz. glass	sl	= slice	tsp	= teaspoon

INDEX